C-4968 CAREER EXAMINATION SERIES

*This is your
PASSBOOK for...*

Evidence and Property Control Specialist

*Test Preparation Study Guide
Questions & Answers*

NATIONAL LEARNING CORPORATION®

COPYRIGHT NOTICE

This book is SOLELY intended for, is sold ONLY to, and its use is RESTRICTED to individual, bona fide applicants or candidates who qualify by virtue of having seriously filed applications for appropriate license, certificate, professional and/or promotional advancement, higher school matriculation, scholarship, or other legitimate requirements of education and/or governmental authorities.

This book is NOT intended for use, class instruction, tutoring, training, duplication, copying, reprinting, excerption, or adaptation, etc., by:

1) Other publishers
2) Proprietors and/or Instructors of "Coaching" and/or Preparatory Courses
3) Personnel and/or Training Divisions of commercial, industrial, and governmental organizations
4) Schools, colleges, or universities and/or their departments and staffs, including teachers and other personnel
5) Testing Agencies or Bureaus
6) Study groups which seek by the purchase of a single volume to copy and/or duplicate and/or adapt this material for use by the group as a whole without having purchased individual volumes for each of the members of the group
7) Et al.

Such persons would be in violation of appropriate Federal and State statutes.

PROVISION OF LICENSING AGREEMENTS – Recognized educational, commercial, industrial, and governmental institutions and organizations, and others legitimately engaged in educational pursuits, including training, testing, and measurement activities, may address request for a licensing agreement to the copyright owners, who will determine whether, and under what conditions, including fees and charges, the materials in this book may be used them. In other words, a licensing facility exists for the legitimate use of the material in this book on other than an individual basis. However, it is asseverated and affirmed here that the material in this book CANNOT be used without the receipt of the express permission of such a licensing agreement from the Publishers. Inquiries re licensing should be addressed to the company, attention rights and permissions department.

All rights reserved, including the right of reproduction in whole or in part, in any form or by any means, electronic or mechanical, including photocopying, recording, or by any information storage and retrieval system, without permission in writing from the Publisher.

Copyright © 2024 by
National Learning Corporation

212 Michael Drive, Syosset, NY 11791
(516) 921-8888 • www.passbooks.com
E-mail: info@passbooks.com

PUBLISHED IN THE UNITED STATES OF AMERICA

PASSBOOK® SERIES

THE *PASSBOOK® SERIES* has been created to prepare applicants and candidates for the ultimate academic battlefield – the examination room.

At some time in our lives, each and every one of us may be required to take an examination – for validation, matriculation, admission, qualification, registration, certification, or licensure.

Based on the assumption that every applicant or candidate has met the basic formal educational standards, has taken the required number of courses, and read the necessary texts, the *PASSBOOK® SERIES* furnishes the one special preparation which may assure passing with confidence, instead of failing with insecurity. Examination questions – together with answers – are furnished as the basic vehicle for study so that the mysteries of the examination and its compounding difficulties may be eliminated or diminished by a sure method.

This book is meant to help you pass your examination provided that you qualify and are serious in your objective.

The entire field is reviewed through the huge store of content information which is succinctly presented through a provocative and challenging approach – the question-and-answer method.

A climate of success is established by furnishing the correct answers at the end of each test.

You soon learn to recognize types of questions, forms of questions, and patterns of questioning. You may even begin to anticipate expected outcomes.

You perceive that many questions are repeated or adapted so that you can gain acute insights, which may enable you to score many sure points.

You learn how to confront new questions, or types of questions, and to attack them confidently and work out the correct answers.

You note objectives and emphases, and recognize pitfalls and dangers, so that you may make positive educational adjustments.

Moreover, you are kept fully informed in relation to new concepts, methods, practices, and directions in the field.

You discover that you are actually taking the examination all the time: you are preparing for the examination by "taking" an examination, not by reading extraneous and/or supererogatory textbooks.

In short, this PASSBOOK®, used directedly, should be an important factor in helping you to pass your test.

EVIDENCE AND PROPERTY CONTROL SPECIALIST

DUTIES
Evidence and Property Control Specialists, under supervision, perform responsible work in performing or supervising security, courier and storage functions for the transport, inspection, storage and delivery of legal and illegal substances and property, such as firearms, narcotics, cash, vehicles, jewelry, etc., being held in evidence by the Police Department or the Office of the Chief Medical Examiner, and the facilities in which they are held. All Evidence and Property Control Specialists perform related work.

SCOPE OF THE EXAMINATION
The multiple-choice test is designed to assess the extent to which candidates have certain abilities determined to be important to the performance of the tasks of an Evidence and Property Control Specialist.

The test may include questions requiring the use of any of the following abilities:

Written Comprehension: understanding written sentences and paragraphs. Example: An Evidence and Property Control Specialist might use this ability when reviewing an invoice or a voucher.

Written Expression: using English words or sentences in writing so that others will understand. Example: An Evidence and Property Control Specialist might use this ability when recording daily logs.

Memorization: remembering information, such as words, numbers, pictures and procedures. Pieces of information can be remembered by themselves or with other pieces of information. Example: An Evidence and Property Control Specialist might use this ability when recalling details on an invoice or voucher.

Problem Sensitivity: being able to tell when something is wrong or is likely to go wrong. It includes being able to identify the whole problem as well as elements of the problem. Example: An Evidence and Property Control Specialist might use this ability when releasing evidence or property to the public.

Number Facility: adding, subtracting, multiplying and dividing quickly and correctly. Example: An Evidence and Property Control Specialist might use this ability when checking money or several pieces of evidence or property.

Information Ordering: following correctly a rule or set of rules or actions in a certain order. The rule or set of rules used must be given. The things or actions to be put in order can include numbers, letters, words, pictures, procedures, sentences, and mathematical or logical operations. Example: An Evidence and Property Control Specialist might use this ability when packaging evidence or property to be sent to other facilities.

Spatial Orientation: is the ability to tell where you are in relation to the location of some object or to tell where the object is in relation to you. Example: An Evidence and Property Control Specialist might use this ability when storing evidence or property in their assigned locations.

Matching: The degree to which one can compare letters, numbers, objects, pictures or patterns accurately. It includes the ability to detect errors, make the appropriate corrections, and recognize similarities in stock materials. Example: An Evidence and Property Control Specialist might use this ability when comparing information from several documents.

Certain questions may need to be answered on the basis of documents or other information supplied to the candidates on the date of the multiple-choice exam.

HOW TO TAKE A TEST

I. YOU MUST PASS AN EXAMINATION

A. *WHAT EVERY CANDIDATE SHOULD KNOW*

Examination applicants often ask us for help in preparing for the written test. What can I study in advance? What kinds of questions will be asked? How will the test be given? How will the papers be graded?

As an applicant for a civil service examination, you may be wondering about some of these things. Our purpose here is to suggest effective methods of advance study and to describe civil service examinations.

Your chances for success on this examination can be increased if you know how to prepare. Those "pre-examination jitters" can be reduced if you know what to expect. You can even experience an adventure in good citizenship if you know why civil service exams are given.

B. *WHY ARE CIVIL SERVICE EXAMINATIONS GIVEN?*

Civil service examinations are important to you in two ways. As a citizen, you want public jobs filled by employees who know how to do their work. As a job seeker, you want a fair chance to compete for that job on an equal footing with other candidates. The best-known means of accomplishing this two-fold goal is the competitive examination.

Exams are widely publicized throughout the nation. They may be administered for jobs in federal, state, city, municipal, town or village governments or agencies.

Any citizen may apply, with some limitations, such as the age or residence of applicants. Your experience and education may be reviewed to see whether you meet the requirements for the particular examination. When these requirements exist, they are reasonable and applied consistently to all applicants. Thus, a competitive examination may cause you some uneasiness now, but it is your privilege and safeguard.

C. *HOW ARE CIVIL SERVICE EXAMS DEVELOPED?*

Examinations are carefully written by trained technicians who are specialists in the field known as "psychological measurement," in consultation with recognized authorities in the field of work that the test will cover. These experts recommend the subject matter areas or skills to be tested; only those knowledges or skills important to your success on the job are included. The most reliable books and source materials available are used as references. Together, the experts and technicians judge the difficulty level of the questions.

Test technicians know how to phrase questions so that the problem is clearly stated. Their ethics do not permit "trick" or "catch" questions. Questions may have been tried out on sample groups, or subjected to statistical analysis, to determine their usefulness.

Written tests are often used in combination with performance tests, ratings of training and experience, and oral interviews. All of these measures combine to form the best-known means of finding the right person for the right job.

II. HOW TO PASS THE WRITTEN TEST

A. NATURE OF THE EXAMINATION

To prepare intelligently for civil service examinations, you should know how they differ from school examinations you have taken. In school you were assigned certain definite pages to read or subjects to cover. The examination questions were quite detailed and usually emphasized memory. Civil service exams, on the other hand, try to discover your present ability to perform the duties of a position, plus your potentiality to learn these duties. In other words, a civil service exam attempts to predict how successful you will be. Questions cover such a broad area that they cannot be as minute and detailed as school exam questions.

In the public service similar kinds of work, or positions, are grouped together in one "class." This process is known as *position-classification*. All the positions in a class are paid according to the salary range for that class. One class title covers all of these positions, and they are all tested by the same examination.

B. FOUR BASIC STEPS

1) Study the announcement

How, then, can you know what subjects to study? Our best answer is: "Learn as much as possible about the class of positions for which you've applied." The exam will test the knowledge, skills and abilities needed to do the work.

Your most valuable source of information about the position you want is the official exam announcement. This announcement lists the training and experience qualifications. Check these standards and apply only if you come reasonably close to meeting them.

The brief description of the position in the examination announcement offers some clues to the subjects which will be tested. Think about the job itself. Review the duties in your mind. Can you perform them, or are there some in which you are rusty? Fill in the blank spots in your preparation.

Many jurisdictions preview the written test in the exam announcement by including a section called "Knowledge and Abilities Required," "Scope of the Examination," or some similar heading. Here you will find out specifically what fields will be tested.

2) Review your own background

Once you learn in general what the position is all about, and what you need to know to do the work, ask yourself which subjects you already know fairly well and which need improvement. You may wonder whether to concentrate on improving your strong areas or on building some background in your fields of weakness. When the announcement has specified "some knowledge" or "considerable knowledge," or has used adjectives like "beginning principles of..." or "advanced ... methods," you can get a clue as to the number and difficulty of questions to be asked in any given field. More questions, and hence broader coverage, would be included for those subjects which are more important in the work. Now weigh your strengths and weaknesses against the job requirements and prepare accordingly.

3) Determine the level of the position

Another way to tell how intensively you should prepare is to understand the level of the job for which you are applying. Is it the entering level? In other words, is this the position in which beginners in a field of work are hired? Or is it an intermediate or advanced level? Sometimes this is indicated by such words as "Junior" or "Senior" in the class title. Other jurisdictions use Roman numerals to designate the level – Clerk I, Clerk II, for example. The word "Supervisor" sometimes appears in the title. If the level is not indicated by the title, check the description of duties. Will you be working under very close supervision, or will you have responsibility for independent decisions in this work?

4) Choose appropriate study materials

Now that you know the subjects to be examined and the relative amount of each subject to be covered, you can choose suitable study materials. For beginning level jobs, or even advanced ones, if you have a pronounced weakness in some aspect of your training, read a modern, standard textbook in that field. Be sure it is up to date and has general coverage. Such books are normally available at your library, and the librarian will be glad to help you locate one. For entry-level positions, questions of appropriate difficulty are chosen – neither highly advanced questions, nor those too simple. Such questions require careful thought but not advanced training.

If the position for which you are applying is technical or advanced, you will read more advanced, specialized material. If you are already familiar with the basic principles of your field, elementary textbooks would waste your time. Concentrate on advanced textbooks and technical periodicals. Think through the concepts and review difficult problems in your field.

These are all general sources. You can get more ideas on your own initiative, following these leads. For example, training manuals and publications of the government agency which employs workers in your field can be useful, particularly for technical and professional positions. A letter or visit to the government department involved may result in more specific study suggestions, and certainly will provide you with a more definite idea of the exact nature of the position you are seeking.

III. KINDS OF TESTS

Tests are used for purposes other than measuring knowledge and ability to perform specified duties. For some positions, it is equally important to test ability to make adjustments to new situations or to profit from training. In others, basic mental abilities not dependent on information are essential. Questions which test these things may not appear as pertinent to the duties of the position as those which test for knowledge and information. Yet they are often highly important parts of a fair examination. For very general questions, it is almost impossible to help you direct your study efforts. What we can do is to point out some of the more common of these general abilities needed in public service positions and describe some typical questions.

1) General information

Broad, general information has been found useful for predicting job success in some kinds of work. This is tested in a variety of ways, from vocabulary lists to questions about current events. Basic background in some field of work, such as sociology or economics, may be sampled in a group of questions. Often these are principles which have become familiar to most persons through exposure rather than through formal training. It is difficult to advise you how to study for these questions; being alert to the world around you is our best suggestion.

2) Verbal ability

An example of an ability needed in many positions is verbal or language ability. Verbal ability is, in brief, the ability to use and understand words. Vocabulary and grammar tests are typical measures of this ability. Reading comprehension or paragraph interpretation questions are common in many kinds of civil service tests. You are given a paragraph of written material and asked to find its central meaning.

3) Numerical ability

Number skills can be tested by the familiar arithmetic problem, by checking paired lists of numbers to see which are alike and which are different, or by interpreting charts and graphs. In the latter test, a graph may be printed in the test booklet which you are asked to use as the basis for answering questions.

4) Observation

A popular test for law-enforcement positions is the observation test. A picture is shown to you for several minutes, then taken away. Questions about the picture test your ability to observe both details and larger elements.

5) Following directions

In many positions in the public service, the employee must be able to carry out written instructions dependably and accurately. You may be given a chart with several columns, each column listing a variety of information. The questions require you to carry out directions involving the information given in the chart.

6) Skills and aptitudes

Performance tests effectively measure some manual skills and aptitudes. When the skill is one in which you are trained, such as typing or shorthand, you can practice. These tests are often very much like those given in business school or high school courses. For many of the other skills and aptitudes, however, no short-time preparation can be made. Skills and abilities natural to you or that you have developed throughout your lifetime are being tested.

Many of the general questions just described provide all the data needed to answer the questions and ask you to use your reasoning ability to find the answers. Your best preparation for these tests, as well as for tests of facts and ideas, is to be at your physical and mental best. You, no doubt, have your own methods of getting into an exam-taking mood and keeping "in shape." The next section lists some ideas on this subject.

IV. KINDS OF QUESTIONS

Only rarely is the "essay" question, which you answer in narrative form, used in civil service tests. Civil service tests are usually of the short-answer type. Full instructions for answering these questions will be given to you at the examination. But in case this is your first experience with short-answer questions and separate answer sheets, here is what you need to know:

1) Multiple-choice Questions

Most popular of the short-answer questions is the "multiple choice" or "best answer" question. It can be used, for example, to test for factual knowledge, ability to solve problems or judgment in meeting situations found at work.

A multiple-choice question is normally one of three types—
- It can begin with an incomplete statement followed by several possible endings. You are to find the one ending which *best* completes the statement, although some of the others may not be entirely wrong.
- It can also be a complete statement in the form of a question which is answered by choosing one of the statements listed.

- It can be in the form of a problem – again you select the best answer.

Here is an example of a multiple-choice question with a discussion which should give you some clues as to the method for choosing the right answer:

When an employee has a complaint about his assignment, the action which will *best* help him overcome his difficulty is to
   A. discuss his difficulty with his coworkers
   B. take the problem to the head of the organization
   C. take the problem to the person who gave him the assignment
   D. say nothing to anyone about his complaint

In answering this question, you should study each of the choices to find which is best. Consider choice "A" – Certainly an employee may discuss his complaint with fellow employees, but no change or improvement can result, and the complaint remains unresolved. Choice "B" is a poor choice since the head of the organization probably does not know what assignment you have been given, and taking your problem to him is known as "going over the head" of the supervisor. The supervisor, or person who made the assignment, is the person who can clarify it or correct any injustice. Choice "C" is, therefore, correct. To say nothing, as in choice "D," is unwise. Supervisors have and interest in knowing the problems employees are facing, and the employee is seeking a solution to his problem.

2) True/False Questions

The "true/false" or "right/wrong" form of question is sometimes used. Here a complete statement is given. Your job is to decide whether the statement is right or wrong.

SAMPLE: A roaming cell-phone call to a nearby city costs less than a non-roaming call to a distant city.

This statement is wrong, or false, since roaming calls are more expensive.

This is not a complete list of all possible question forms, although most of the others are variations of these common types. You will always get complete directions for answering questions. Be sure you understand *how* to mark your answers – ask questions until you do.

V. RECORDING YOUR ANSWERS

Computer terminals are used more and more today for many different kinds of exams.

For an examination with very few applicants, you may be told to record your answers in the test booklet itself. Separate answer sheets are much more common. If this separate answer sheet is to be scored by machine – and this is often the case – it is highly important that you mark your answers correctly in order to get credit.

An electronic scoring machine is often used in civil service offices because of the speed with which papers can be scored. Machine-scored answer sheets must be marked with a pencil, which will be given to you. This pencil has a high graphite content which responds to the electronic scoring machine. As a matter of fact, stray dots may register as answers, so do not let your pencil rest on the answer sheet while you are pondering the correct answer. Also, if your pencil lead breaks or is otherwise defective, ask for another.

Since the answer sheet will be dropped in a slot in the scoring machine, be careful not to bend the corners or get the paper crumpled.

The answer sheet normally has five vertical columns of numbers, with 30 numbers to a column. These numbers correspond to the question numbers in your test booklet. After each number, going across the page are four or five pairs of dotted lines. These short dotted lines have small letters or numbers above them. The first two pairs may also have a "T" or "F" above the letters. This indicates that the first two pairs only are to be used if the questions are of the true-false type. If the questions are multiple choice, disregard the "T" and "F" and pay attention only to the small letters or numbers.

Answer your questions in the manner of the sample that follows:

32. The largest city in the United States is
    A. Washington, D.C.
    B. New York City
    C. Chicago
    D. Detroit
    E. San Francisco

1) Choose the answer you think is best. (New York City is the largest, so "B" is correct.)
2) Find the row of dotted lines numbered the same as the question you are answering. (Find row number 32)
3) Find the pair of dotted lines corresponding to the answer. (Find the pair of lines under the mark "B.")
4) Make a solid black mark between the dotted lines.

VI. BEFORE THE TEST

Common sense will help you find procedures to follow to get ready for an examination. Too many of us, however, overlook these sensible measures. Indeed, nervousness and fatigue have been found to be the most serious reasons why applicants fail to do their best on civil service tests. Here is a list of reminders:

- Begin your preparation early – Don't wait until the last minute to go scurrying around for books and materials or to find out what the position is all about.
- Prepare continuously – An hour a night for a week is better than an all-night cram session. This has been definitely established. What is more, a night a week for a month will return better dividends than crowding your study into a shorter period of time.
- Locate the place of the exam – You have been sent a notice telling you when and where to report for the examination. If the location is in a different town or otherwise unfamiliar to you, it would be well to inquire the best route and learn something about the building.
- Relax the night before the test – Allow your mind to rest. Do not study at all that night. Plan some mild recreation or diversion; then go to bed early and get a good night's sleep.
- Get up early enough to make a leisurely trip to the place for the test – This way unforeseen events, traffic snarls, unfamiliar buildings, etc. will not upset you.
- Dress comfortably – A written test is not a fashion show. You will be known by number and not by name, so wear something comfortable.

- Leave excess paraphernalia at home – Shopping bags and odd bundles will get in your way. You need bring only the items mentioned in the official notice you received; usually everything you need is provided. Do not bring reference books to the exam. They will only confuse those last minutes and be taken away from you when in the test room.
- Arrive somewhat ahead of time – If because of transportation schedules you must get there very early, bring a newspaper or magazine to take your mind off yourself while waiting.
- Locate the examination room – When you have found the proper room, you will be directed to the seat or part of the room where you will sit. Sometimes you are given a sheet of instructions to read while you are waiting. Do not fill out any forms until you are told to do so; just read them and be prepared.
- Relax and prepare to listen to the instructions
- If you have any physical problem that may keep you from doing your best, be sure to tell the test administrator. If you are sick or in poor health, you really cannot do your best on the exam. You can come back and take the test some other time.

VII. AT THE TEST

The day of the test is here and you have the test booklet in your hand. The temptation to get going is very strong. Caution! There is more to success than knowing the right answers. You must know how to identify your papers and understand variations in the type of short-answer question used in this particular examination. Follow these suggestions for maximum results from your efforts:

1) Cooperate with the monitor

The test administrator has a duty to create a situation in which you can be as much at ease as possible. He will give instructions, tell you when to begin, check to see that you are marking your answer sheet correctly, and so on. He is not there to guard you, although he will see that your competitors do not take unfair advantage. He wants to help you do your best.

2) Listen to all instructions

Don't jump the gun! Wait until you understand all directions. In most civil service tests you get more time than you need to answer the questions. So don't be in a hurry. Read each word of instructions until you clearly understand the meaning. Study the examples, listen to all announcements and follow directions. Ask questions if you do not understand what to do.

3) Identify your papers

Civil service exams are usually identified by number only. You will be assigned a number; you must not put your name on your test papers. Be sure to copy your number correctly. Since more than one exam may be given, copy your exact examination title.

4) Plan your time

Unless you are told that a test is a "speed" or "rate of work" test, speed itself is usually not important. Time enough to answer all the questions will be provided, but this does not mean that you have all day. An overall time limit has been set. Divide the total time (in minutes) by the number of questions to determine the approximate time you have for each question.

5) Do not linger over difficult questions

If you come across a difficult question, mark it with a paper clip (useful to have along) and come back to it when you have been through the booklet. One caution if you do this – be sure to skip a number on your answer sheet as well. Check often to be sure that you have not lost your place and that you are marking in the row numbered the same as the question you are answering.

6) Read the questions

Be sure you know what the question asks! Many capable people are unsuccessful because they failed to *read* the questions correctly.

7) Answer all questions

Unless you have been instructed that a penalty will be deducted for incorrect answers, it is better to guess than to omit a question.

8) Speed tests

It is often better NOT to guess on speed tests. It has been found that on timed tests people are tempted to spend the last few seconds before time is called in marking answers at random – without even reading them – in the hope of picking up a few extra points. To discourage this practice, the instructions may warn you that your score will be "corrected" for guessing. That is, a penalty will be applied. The incorrect answers will be deducted from the correct ones, or some other penalty formula will be used.

9) Review your answers

If you finish before time is called, go back to the questions you guessed or omitted to give them further thought. Review other answers if you have time.

10) Return your test materials

If you are ready to leave before others have finished or time is called, take ALL your materials to the monitor and leave quietly. Never take any test material with you. The monitor can discover whose papers are not complete, and taking a test booklet may be grounds for disqualification.

VIII. EXAMINATION TECHNIQUES

1) Read the general instructions carefully. These are usually printed on the first page of the exam booklet. As a rule, these instructions refer to the timing of the examination; the fact that you should not start work until the signal and must stop work at a signal, etc. If there are any *special* instructions, such as a choice of questions to be answered, make sure that you note this instruction carefully.

2) When you are ready to start work on the examination, that is as soon as the signal has been given, read the instructions to each question booklet, underline any key words or phrases, such as *least, best, outline, describe* and the like. In this way you will tend to answer as requested rather than discover on reviewing your paper that you *listed without describing*, that you selected the *worst* choice rather than the *best* choice, etc.

3) If the examination is of the objective or multiple-choice type – that is, each question will also give a series of possible answers: A, B, C or D, and you are called upon to select the best answer and write the letter next to that answer on your answer paper – it is advisable to start answering each question in turn. There may be anywhere from 50 to 100 such questions in the three or four hours allotted and you can see how much time would be taken if you read through all the questions before beginning to answer any. Furthermore, if you come across a question or group of questions which you know would be difficult to answer, it would undoubtedly affect your handling of all the other questions.

4) If the examination is of the essay type and contains but a few questions, it is a moot point as to whether you should read all the questions before starting to answer any one. Of course, if you are given a choice – say five out of seven and the like – then it is essential to read all the questions so you can eliminate the two that are most difficult. If, however, you are asked to answer all the questions, there may be danger in trying to answer the easiest one first because you may find that you will spend too much time on it. The best technique is to answer the first question, then proceed to the second, etc.

5) Time your answers. Before the exam begins, write down the time it started, then add the time allowed for the examination and write down the time it must be completed, then divide the time available somewhat as follows:
   - If 3-1/2 hours are allowed, that would be 210 minutes. If you have 80 objective-type questions, that would be an average of 2-1/2 minutes per question. Allow yourself no more than 2 minutes per question, or a total of 160 minutes, which will permit about 50 minutes to review.
   - If for the time allotment of 210 minutes there are 7 essay questions to answer, that would average about 30 minutes a question. Give yourself only 25 minutes per question so that you have about 35 minutes to review.

6) The most important instruction is to *read each question* and make sure you know what is wanted. The second most important instruction is to *time yourself properly* so that you answer every question. The third most important instruction is to *answer every question*. Guess if you have to but include something for each question. Remember that you will receive no credit for a blank and will probably receive some credit if you write something in answer to an essay question. If you guess a letter – say "B" for a multiple-choice question – you may have guessed right. If you leave a blank as an answer to a multiple-choice question, the examiners may respect your feelings but it will not add a point to your score. Some exams may penalize you for wrong answers, so in such cases *only*, you may not want to guess unless you have some basis for your answer.

7) Suggestions
   a. Objective-type questions
      1. Examine the question booklet for proper sequence of pages and questions
      2. Read all instructions carefully
      3. Skip any question which seems too difficult; return to it after all other questions have been answered
      4. Apportion your time properly; do not spend too much time on any single question or group of questions

5. Note and underline key words – *all, most, fewest, least, best, worst, same, opposite*, etc.
6. Pay particular attention to negatives
7. Note unusual option, e.g., unduly long, short, complex, different or similar in content to the body of the question
8. Observe the use of "hedging" words – *probably, may, most likely*, etc.
9. Make sure that your answer is put next to the same number as the question
10. Do not second-guess unless you have good reason to believe the second answer is definitely more correct
11. Cross out original answer if you decide another answer is more accurate; do not erase until you are ready to hand your paper in
12. Answer all questions; guess unless instructed otherwise
13. Leave time for review

b. Essay questions
1. Read each question carefully
2. Determine exactly what is wanted. Underline key words or phrases.
3. Decide on outline or paragraph answer
4. Include many different points and elements unless asked to develop any one or two points or elements
5. Show impartiality by giving pros and cons unless directed to select one side only
6. Make and write down any assumptions you find necessary to answer the questions
7. Watch your English, grammar, punctuation and choice of words
8. Time your answers; don't crowd material

8) Answering the essay question

Most essay questions can be answered by framing the specific response around several key words or ideas. Here are a few such key words or ideas:

M's: manpower, materials, methods, money, management
P's: purpose, program, policy, plan, procedure, practice, problems, pitfalls, personnel, public relations

a. Six basic steps in handling problems:
1. Preliminary plan and background development
2. Collect information, data and facts
3. Analyze and interpret information, data and facts
4. Analyze and develop solutions as well as make recommendations
5. Prepare report and sell recommendations
6. Install recommendations and follow up effectiveness

b. Pitfalls to avoid
1. *Taking things for granted* – A statement of the situation does not necessarily imply that each of the elements is necessarily true; for example, a complaint may be invalid and biased so that all that can be taken for granted is that a complaint has been registered

2. *Considering only one side of a situation* – Wherever possible, indicate several alternatives and then point out the reasons you selected the best one
3. *Failing to indicate follow up* – Whenever your answer indicates action on your part, make certain that you will take proper follow-up action to see how successful your recommendations, procedures or actions turn out to be
4. *Taking too long in answering any single question* – Remember to time your answers properly

IX. AFTER THE TEST

Scoring procedures differ in detail among civil service jurisdictions although the general principles are the same. Whether the papers are hand-scored or graded by machine we have described, they are nearly always graded by number. That is, the person who marks the paper knows only the number – never the name – of the applicant. Not until all the papers have been graded will they be matched with names. If other tests, such as training and experience or oral interview ratings have been given, scores will be combined. Different parts of the examination usually have different weights. For example, the written test might count 60 percent of the final grade, and a rating of training and experience 40 percent. In many jurisdictions, veterans will have a certain number of points added to their grades.

After the final grade has been determined, the names are placed in grade order and an eligible list is established. There are various methods for resolving ties between those who get the same final grade – probably the most common is to place first the name of the person whose application was received first. Job offers are made from the eligible list in the order the names appear on it. You will be notified of your grade and your rank as soon as all these computations have been made. This will be done as rapidly as possible.

People who are found to meet the requirements in the announcement are called "eligibles." Their names are put on a list of eligible candidates. An eligible's chances of getting a job depend on how high he stands on this list and how fast agencies are filling jobs from the list.

When a job is to be filled from a list of eligibles, the agency asks for the names of people on the list of eligibles for that job. When the civil service commission receives this request, it sends to the agency the names of the three people highest on this list. Or, if the job to be filled has specialized requirements, the office sends the agency the names of the top three persons who meet these requirements from the general list.

The appointing officer makes a choice from among the three people whose names were sent to him. If the selected person accepts the appointment, the names of the others are put back on the list to be considered for future openings.

That is the rule in hiring from all kinds of eligible lists, whether they are for typist, carpenter, chemist, or something else. For every vacancy, the appointing officer has his choice of any one of the top three eligibles on the list. This explains why the person whose name is on top of the list sometimes does not get an appointment when some of the persons lower on the list do. If the appointing officer chooses the second or third eligible, the No. 1 eligible does not get a job at once, but stays on the list until he is appointed or the list is terminated.

X. HOW TO PASS THE INTERVIEW TEST

The examination for which you applied requires an oral interview test. You have already taken the written test and you are now being called for the interview test – the final part of the formal examination.

You may think that it is not possible to prepare for an interview test and that there are no procedures to follow during an interview. Our purpose is to point out some things you can do in advance that will help you and some good rules to follow and pitfalls to avoid while you are being interviewed.

What is an interview supposed to test?

The written examination is designed to test the technical knowledge and competence of the candidate; the oral is designed to evaluate intangible qualities, not readily measured otherwise, and to establish a list showing the relative fitness of each candidate – as measured against his competitors – for the position sought. Scoring is not on the basis of "right" and "wrong," but on a sliding scale of values ranging from "not passable" to "outstanding." As a matter of fact, it is possible to achieve a relatively low score without a single "incorrect" answer because of evident weakness in the qualities being measured.

Occasionally, an examination may consist entirely of an oral test – either an individual or a group oral. In such cases, information is sought concerning the technical knowledges and abilities of the candidate, since there has been no written examination for this purpose. More commonly, however, an oral test is used to supplement a written examination.

Who conducts interviews?

The composition of oral boards varies among different jurisdictions. In nearly all, a representative of the personnel department serves as chairman. One of the members of the board may be a representative of the department in which the candidate would work. In some cases, "outside experts" are used, and, frequently, a businessman or some other representative of the general public is asked to serve. Labor and management or other special groups may be represented. The aim is to secure the services of experts in the appropriate field.

However the board is composed, it is a good idea (and not at all improper or unethical) to ascertain in advance of the interview who the members are and what groups they represent. When you are introduced to them, you will have some idea of their backgrounds and interests, and at least you will not stutter and stammer over their names.

What should be done before the interview?

While knowledge about the board members is useful and takes some of the surprise element out of the interview, there is other preparation which is more substantive. It *is* possible to prepare for an oral interview – in several ways:

1) Keep a copy of your application and review it carefully before the interview

This may be the only document before the oral board, and the starting point of the interview. Know what education and experience you have listed there, and the sequence and dates of all of it. Sometimes the board will ask you to review the highlights of your experience for them; you should not have to hem and haw doing it.

2) Study the class specification and the examination announcement

Usually, the oral board has one or both of these to guide them. The qualities, characteristics or knowledges required by the position sought are stated in these documents. They offer valuable clues as to the nature of the oral interview. For example, if the job involves supervisory responsibilities, the announcement will usually indicate that knowledge of modern supervisory methods and the qualifications of the candidate as a supervisor will be tested. If so, you can expect such questions, frequently in the form of a hypothetical situation which you are expected to solve. NEVER go into an oral without knowledge of the duties and responsibilities of the job you seek.

3) Think through each qualification required

Try to visualize the kind of questions you would ask if you were a board member. How well could you answer them? Try especially to appraise your own knowledge and background in each area, *measured against the job sought*, and identify any areas in which you are weak. Be critical and realistic – do not flatter yourself.

4) Do some general reading in areas in which you feel you may be weak

For example, if the job involves supervision and your past experience has NOT, some general reading in supervisory methods and practices, particularly in the field of human relations, might be useful. Do NOT study agency procedures or detailed manuals. The oral board will be testing your understanding and capacity, not your memory.

5) Get a good night's sleep and watch your general health and mental attitude

You will want a clear head at the interview. Take care of a cold or any other minor ailment, and of course, no hangovers.

What should be done on the day of the interview?

Now comes the day of the interview itself. Give yourself plenty of time to get there. Plan to arrive somewhat ahead of the scheduled time, particularly if your appointment is in the fore part of the day. If a previous candidate fails to appear, the board might be ready for you a bit early. By early afternoon an oral board is almost invariably behind schedule if there are many candidates, and you may have to wait. Take along a book or magazine to read, or your application to review, but leave any extraneous material in the waiting room when you go in for your interview. In any event, relax and compose yourself.

The matter of dress is important. The board is forming impressions about you – from your experience, your manners, your attitude, and your appearance. Give your personal appearance careful attention. Dress your best, but not your flashiest. Choose conservative, appropriate clothing, and be sure it is immaculate. This is a business interview, and your appearance should indicate that you regard it as such. Besides, being well groomed and properly dressed will help boost your confidence.

Sooner or later, someone will call your name and escort you into the interview room. *This is it.* From here on you are on your own. It is too late for any more preparation. But remember, you asked for this opportunity to prove your fitness, and you are here because your request was granted.

What happens when you go in?

The usual sequence of events will be as follows: The clerk (who is often the board stenographer) will introduce you to the chairman of the oral board, who will introduce you to the other members of the board. Acknowledge the introductions before you sit down. Do not be surprised if you find a microphone facing you or a stenotypist sitting by. Oral interviews are usually recorded in the event of an appeal or other review.

Usually the chairman of the board will open the interview by reviewing the highlights of your education and work experience from your application – primarily for the benefit of the other members of the board, as well as to get the material into the record. Do not interrupt or comment unless there is an error or significant misinterpretation; if that is the case, do not hesitate. But do not quibble about insignificant matters. Also, he will usually ask you some question about your education, experience or your present job – partly to get you to start talking and to establish the interviewing "rapport." He may start the actual questioning, or turn it over to one of the other members. Frequently, each member undertakes the questioning on a particular area, one in which he is perhaps most competent, so you can expect each member to participate in the examination. Because time is limited, you may also expect some rather abrupt switches in the direction the questioning takes, so do not be upset by it. Normally, a board member will not pursue a single line of questioning unless he discovers a particular strength or weakness.

After each member has participated, the chairman will usually ask whether any member has any further questions, then will ask you if you have anything you wish to add. Unless you are expecting this question, it may floor you. Worse, it may start you off on an extended, extemporaneous speech. The board is not usually seeking more information. The question is principally to offer you a last opportunity to present further qualifications or to indicate that you have nothing to add. So, if you feel that a significant qualification or characteristic has been overlooked, it is proper to point it out in a sentence or so. Do not compliment the board on the thoroughness of their examination – they have been sketchy, and you know it. If you wish, merely say, "No thank you, I have nothing further to add." This is a point where you can "talk yourself out" of a good impression or fail to present an important bit of information. Remember, *you close the interview yourself*.

The chairman will then say, "That is all, Mr. _____, thank you." Do not be startled; the interview is over, and quicker than you think. Thank him, gather your belongings and take your leave. Save your sigh of relief for the other side of the door.

How to put your best foot forward

Throughout this entire process, you may feel that the board individually and collectively is trying to pierce your defenses, seek out your hidden weaknesses and embarrass and confuse you. Actually, this is not true. They are obliged to make an appraisal of your qualifications for the job you are seeking, and they want to see you in your best light. Remember, they must interview all candidates and a non-cooperative candidate may become a failure in spite of their best efforts to bring out his qualifications. Here are 15 suggestions that will help you:

1) Be natural – Keep your attitude confident, not cocky

If you are not confident that you can do the job, do not expect the board to be. Do not apologize for your weaknesses, try to bring out your strong points. The board is interested in a positive, not negative, presentation. Cockiness will antagonize any board member and make him wonder if you are covering up a weakness by a false show of strength.

2) Get comfortable, but don't lounge or sprawl

Sit erectly but not stiffly. A careless posture may lead the board to conclude that you are careless in other things, or at least that you are not impressed by the importance of the occasion. Either conclusion is natural, even if incorrect. Do not fuss with your clothing, a pencil or an ashtray. Your hands may occasionally be useful to emphasize a point; do not let them become a point of distraction.

3) Do not wisecrack or make small talk

This is a serious situation, and your attitude should show that you consider it as such. Further, the time of the board is limited – they do not want to waste it, and neither should you.

4) Do not exaggerate your experience or abilities

In the first place, from information in the application or other interviews and sources, the board may know more about you than you think. Secondly, you probably will not get away with it. An experienced board is rather adept at spotting such a situation, so do not take the chance.

5) If you know a board member, do not make a point of it, yet do not hide it

Certainly you are not fooling him, and probably not the other members of the board. Do not try to take advantage of your acquaintanceship – it will probably do you little good.

6) Do not dominate the interview

Let the board do that. They will give you the clues – do not assume that you have to do all the talking. Realize that the board has a number of questions to ask you, and do not try to take up all the interview time by showing off your extensive knowledge of the answer to the first one.

7) Be attentive

You only have 20 minutes or so, and you should keep your attention at its sharpest throughout. When a member is addressing a problem or question to you, give him your undivided attention. Address your reply principally to him, but do not exclude the other board members.

8) Do not interrupt

A board member may be stating a problem for you to analyze. He will ask you a question when the time comes. Let him state the problem, and wait for the question.

9) Make sure you understand the question

Do not try to answer until you are sure what the question is. If it is not clear, restate it in your own words or ask the board member to clarify it for you. However, do not haggle about minor elements.

10) Reply promptly but not hastily

A common entry on oral board rating sheets is "candidate responded readily," or "candidate hesitated in replies." Respond as promptly and quickly as you can, but do not jump to a hasty, ill-considered answer.

11) Do not be peremptory in your answers

A brief answer is proper – but do not fire your answer back. That is a losing game from your point of view. The board member can probably ask questions much faster than you can answer them.

12) Do not try to create the answer you think the board member wants

He is interested in what kind of mind you have and how it works – not in playing games. Furthermore, he can usually spot this practice and will actually grade you down on it.

13) Do not switch sides in your reply merely to agree with a board member

Frequently, a member will take a contrary position merely to draw you out and to see if you are willing and able to defend your point of view. Do not start a debate, yet do not surrender a good position. If a position is worth taking, it is worth defending.

14) Do not be afraid to admit an error in judgment if you are shown to be wrong

The board knows that you are forced to reply without any opportunity for careful consideration. Your answer may be demonstrably wrong. If so, admit it and get on with the interview.

15) Do not dwell at length on your present job

The opening question may relate to your present assignment. Answer the question but do not go into an extended discussion. You are being examined for a *new* job, not your present one. As a matter of fact, try to phrase ALL your answers in terms of the job for which you are being examined.

Basis of Rating

Probably you will forget most of these "do's" and "don'ts" when you walk into the oral interview room. Even remembering them all will not ensure you a passing grade. Perhaps you did not have the qualifications in the first place. But remembering them will help you to put your best foot forward, without treading on the toes of the board members.

Rumor and popular opinion to the contrary notwithstanding, an oral board wants you to make the best appearance possible. They know you are under pressure – but they also want to see how you respond to it as a guide to what your reaction would be under the pressures of the job you seek. They will be influenced by the degree of poise you display, the personal traits you show and the manner in which you respond.

ABOUT THIS BOOK

This book contains tests divided into Examination Sections. Go through each test, answering every question in the margin. We have also attached a sample answer sheet at the back of the book that can be removed and used. At the end of each test look at the answer key and check your answers. On the ones you got wrong, look at the right answer choice and learn. Do not fill in the answers first. Do not memorize the questions and answers, but understand the answer and principles involved. On your test, the questions will likely be different from the samples. Questions are changed and new ones added. If you understand these past questions you should have success with any changes that arise. Tests may consist of several types of questions. We have additional books on each subject should more study be advisable or necessary for you. Finally, the more you study, the better prepared you will be. This book is intended to be the last thing you study before you walk into the examination room. Prior study of relevant texts is also recommended. NLC publishes some of these in our Fundamental Series. Knowledge and good sense are important factors in passing your exam. Good luck also helps. So now study this Passbook, absorb the material contained within and take that knowledge into the examination. Then do your best to pass that exam.

EXAMINATION SECTION

EXAMINATION SECTION
TEST 1

DIRECTIONS: Each question or incomplete statement is followed by several suggested answers or completions. Select the one the BEST answers the question or completes the statement. *PRINT THE LETTER OF THE CORRECT ANSWER IN THE SPACE AT THE RIGHT.*

1. The type of property/evidence that is most likely to involve the "two person" rule for handling is

     A. currency
     B. firearms
     C. flammable material
     D. biohazardous material

    1._____

2. An affidavit is most likely to be required in a record for

     A. found property
     B. property seized by search warrant
     C. property held for safekeeping
     D. recovered property

    2._____

3. "Temporary storage" refers to the

     A. gap between the time the employee who seized the property leaves it at the station, and the time that it is actually received by a property room employee
     B. gap between the time an item is signed out for disposition and the time that it is actually disposed of
     C. time during which non-evidentiary property is placed in the custody of a law enforcement agency for temporary protection on behalf of the owner
     D. span of any applicable statute of limitations that impacts the amount of time an item is required to remain in custody

    3._____

4. When storing audio- or videotapes and computer disks, it's important to remember that air, heat, moisture, and magnetism may deteriorate these items within

     A. 6-8 months
     B. 1-2 years
     C. 5-6 years
     D. 10-12 years

    4._____

5. A standard property/evidence record should include
     I. date/time collected/submitted
     II. special instructions
     III. chain of custody
     IV. storage location

     A. I only
     B. I and III
     C. I, II and III
     D. I, II, III and IV

    5._____

6. Biological materials must be in a sealed/container or bag

   A. if they are in transit
   B. only if they are to be used as evidence
   C. at all times
   D. if they are going to be tested again

7. Ideally, the outdoor "bulk area" of a property/evidence section would contain
      I.   automobiles
      II. flammable materials
      III. firearms
      IV. bicycles

   A. I only
   B. I and IV
   C. I, II and IV
   D. I, II, III and IV

8. Materials and supplies used by the property/evidence section should be kept in the

   A. evidence review room
   B. general property/evidence storage area
   C. departmental office
   D. storage area separate from the entire section's facilities

9. Generally, inventories of property/evidence sections should be completed

   A. every three months
   B. every six months
   C. annually
   D. every two years

10. During an inventory, a property specialist comes across an item on the shelf that is not documented anywhere in department records. The item should be listed on a(n)

    A. found property report
    B. disposition form
    C. unable to locate file
    D. right of refusal

11. When fingerprints on an item may be relevant and are a possibility, the item should be

    A. dusted for prints
    B. stored at room temperature
    C. frozen
    D. refrigerated

12. Guidelines for firearms storage include
       I.   room should be alarmed independent of regular intrusion alarm system
       II. weapons should be secured in a manner that makes them impossible to fire
       III. weapons recovered from an underwater location should be cleaned
       IV. generally, firearms to be submitted for forensic processing should be packaged in an airtight container

A. I and II
B. II only
C. I, II and III
D. I, II, III and IV

13. What is the term for non-evidentiary property which, after coming into the custody of a law enforcement agency, has been determined to be lost or abandoned and is not known or suspected to be connected with any criminal offense?

    A. Property for safekeeping
    B. Found property
    C. Property for disposition
    D. Recovered property

14. Within a property/evidence section, narcotics which are most susceptible to theft from within the department are those which have

    A. just been signed off for disposition
    B. not yet been entered into evidence
    C. just been entered into evidence
    D. logged and stored indefinitely

15. Liquid items of biological samples, such as tubes of blood, that are meant to be tested again should be

    A. dried first, then stored at room temperature
    B. stored in refrigerator temperatures of 36-50 degrees Fahrenheit
    C. stored in freezer temperatures of below 32 degrees Fahrenheit
    D. vacuum-sealed, then stored at room temperature

16. For the handling, storage, and maintenance of high-profile items (narcotics, biological materials, firearms, currency, etc.), guidelines include each of the following, EXCEPT

    A. vaults should be constructed of concrete or block
    B. storage should be an exception to the overall property room location and scheme
    C. locking mechanisms should be designed so that two people are needed for entry
    D. alarm systems should consist of an intrusion alarm with door contacts and motion sensors

17. From the property specialist's standpoint, which of the following types of narcotics has different packaging requirements from most other kinds of drugs?

    A. partially processed methamphetamine
    B. cocaine
    C. green marijuana
    D. PCP

18. The original documentation of a property/evidence section inventory would be BEST kept

    A. with the records of the property/evidence section records
    B. with the agency's records bureau
    C. in a high-security area such as the firearms cabinet
    D. in the property supervisor/captain's office

19. Evidence stored with a property/evidence section may be disposed of if
    I. it poses a physical hazard
    II. it is found property with unknown origins
    III. the case is subject to DA refiling
    IV. the case has multiple defendants

    A. I only
    B. I and III
    C. III only
    D. III and IV

20. Any property or evidence submitted to the property/evidence section should have an envelope, tag, or label affixed to it, usually corresponding with the _____ listed on the record.

    A. submitting officer
    B. case number
    C. classification
    D. item number

21. Which of the following is a guideline for the storage of computers?

    A. Disks and other storage media should be detached and stored separately.
    B. They should be stored in a covered outdoor bulk area.
    C. Towers should be stored in the position they were used in.
    D. They should be tightly sealed in metal containers.

22. Most appropriately, a departmental review of property/evidence for disposition would consist of

    A. basing disposition of statutes of limitations
    B. a complete inventory every 6 months-1 year
    C. a review of all criminal cases every 6 months-1 year
    D. an external audit of the efficiency with which space is being used

23. A standard currency envelope should contain each of the following, EXCEPT a

    A. space for witness verification
    B. space for the initials and the ID number of the person seizing and counting the currency
    C. line for the name of additional owners/suspects whose cash is also included in the envelope
    D. register of currency and coins in the envelope, by denomination

24. Guidelines for recording and storing narcotics include
    I. weights should be specified with (gross total weight) or without (net weight) packaging material
    II. after sealing the package, the only staff who should be authorized to re-open it are lab staff
    III. most narcotics should be stored in a heat-sealed plastic bag
    IV. scales used should be recalibrated at least twice a year

    A. I only
    B. I and II

C. I, II and IV
D. I, II, III and IV

25. It's important to note, prior to disposition, that _____ can be considered hazardous waste because of the chemicals used to manufacture them. 25._____

   A. television sets
   B. computer circuit boards
   C. computer hard drives
   D. firearms

KEY (CORRECT ANSWERS)

1.	A	11.	B
2.	A	12.	A
3.	A	13.	B
4.	C	14.	A
5.	D	15.	B
6.	A	16.	B
7.	C	17.	C
8.	D	18.	B
9.	C	19.	A
10.	A	20.	D

21. C
22. C
23. C
24. D
25. B

TEST 2

DIRECTIONS: Each question or incomplete statement is followed by several suggested answers or completions. Select the one the BEST answers the question or completes the statement. *PRINT THE LETTER OF THE CORRECT ANSWER IN THE SPACE AT THE RIGHT.*

1. The best method for marking a firearm is to attach an identification tag to the   1._____

    A. hammer
    B. checkered portion of the grip
    C. barrel
    D. trigger guard

2. "Chain of custody" of an item of evidence is usually considered to have been initiated by the   2._____

    A. property/evidence specialist
    B. original owner
    C. involved party
    D. recovering/reporting officer

3. Generally, the last item to appear on a standard property/evidence record is   3._____

    A. disposition
    B. involved party name
    C. storage location
    D. submitting officer/employee

4. The primary purpose of a property/evidence room inventory is to   4._____

    A. ensure continuity of custody
    B. provide quality control for departmental operations
    C. account for every single item of property
    D. streamline processes

5. The "Big Three" of in-custody property, which require extra protection, security, and handling precautions, include each of the following, EXCEPT   5._____

    A. firearms
    B. biohazardous materials
    C. narcotics
    D. currency

6. Probably the single most important factor in making the operation of a property/evidence section more efficient is   6._____

    A. commingling of different types of evidence in the same area
    B. packaging standards
    C. statutes of limitations
    D. transfer protocols

7. Bloody evidence, or evidence contaminated with other body fluids, should be dried in a controlled, secure environment. Once dried, the items are best stored in   7._____

A. airtight plastic
B. paper bags
C. the open air
D. tightly-wrapped foil

8. If not a separate department within a law enforcement agency, the property/evidence function is most appropriately placed under the authority of

   A. support services/administration
   B. investigations division
   C. property crimes division
   D. uniform division

9. A submitting officer presents a sealed currency envelope to a property specialist without an accompanying verification signature. The property specialist should

   A. ask the officer to list the currency and coin by denomination
   B. open the envelope and count the currency in order to provide corroboration
   C. immediately transfer the currency to the general fund or finance department
   D. exercise right of refusal

10. Containers used to store audio- or videotapes or computer disks should be each of the following, EXCEPT

    A. airtight
    B. water-tight
    C. metallic
    D. non-static

11. Guidelines for conducting property/evidence section inventories include
    I. begin random inventories only from easy-to-describe locations
    II. if possible, conduct the inventory from paper to shelf
    III. if possible, avoid breaking evidence seals to verify contents
    IV. inventories of narcotics signed out for destruction should include random testing to determine purity

    A. I only
    B. I, III and IV
    C. II and III
    D. III and IV

12. When fireworks that have been stored with a property/evidence section are ready for disposal, the most appropriate agency for the job is the

    A. law enforcement agency that held them
    B. Federal Bureau of Investigation
    C. local fire department
    D. federal ATF bureau

13. Guidelines for the storage of flammable materials include
    I. fire extinguishers or sprinkler systems should be available in the storage area
    II. storage in a metal container

III. storage in an airtight container
IV. if possible, storage outside the property room

A. I only
B. I and II
C. I, II and III
D. I, II, III and IV

14. During an inventory, the seal on an envelope is broken. Which of the following is true?

A. Any property contained within the envelope must now be destroyed.
B. The contents must be verified and documented prior to resealing.
C. The contents of the envelope are no longer admissible as evidence.
D. The replacement seal does not require a witness.

15. For narcotic evidence not taken into custody or destroyed at the scene, the recommended documentation method is

A. photographs taken prior to destruction
B. small (.5 mg) samples taken and filed into envelopes
C. an affidavit filed by the collecting officer and witnessed by the property specialist as to the type and amount of substance
D. a simple written description filed with property/evidence section records

16. Unless disposal release is explicitly ordered, property/evidence from _____ should be held indefinitely.
I. falsification of public documents
II. embezzlement of public funds
III. felony sexual offenses
IV. capital homicides

A. I and II
B. I, II and IV
C. III and IV
D. IV only

17. To balance a desire to maximize a return on budgetary resources with the likelihood of future obsolescence, a property/evidence section should keep a minimum of about _____'s worth of forms (records, transfers, etc.) in stock.

A. 3 months
B. 6 months
C. 1 year
D. 3 years

18. Which of the following is LEAST likely to be accepted into a property room as evidence for storage?

A. Bicycle
B. Hypodermic syringe
C. Currency
D. Alcoholic beverage container

19. Bar coding systems, if used in a property/evidence records system, should allow for
    I. password security
    II. validation against the host system
    III. on-demand label printing
    IV. data collection programs for portable terminals

    A. I and II
    B. II only
    C. II, III and IV
    D. I, II, III and IV

20. The most efficient and trouble-free way to inventory a property/ evidence section is to
    A. inventory different types of items at specific times of the year
    B. work only from active case files
    C. perform the inventory all at once at the beginning of each year
    D. consult records only, without looking through individual items

21. When planning or adjusting the layout for a property/evidence storage area, it's important to remember that property for safekeeping
    A. should be commingled with non-quarantined evidence
    B. requires its own separate ventilation system
    C. needs quick, open access and close proximity to the public counter
    D. should be placed on special shelving

22. The most significant factor influencing a property specialist's decision to dispose of property or evidence is likely to be
    A. civil litigation risk
    B. auditing/inventory time
    C. space limitations
    D. increasing potential for misplacing items

23. Transfer forms used by property/evidence sections should NOT
    A. include a brief description
    B. indicate to whom the property was released
    C. name the intended destination
    D. be fastened to the original paperwork while in transit

24. Biological materials that are dried stains, and that are meant to be tested again, should be stored
    A. in the open air
    B. in an airtight container at room temperature
    C. in refrigerator temperatures of 36-50 degrees Fahrenheit
    D. in freezer temperatures of below 32 degrees Fahrenheit

25. A law enforcement agency has discovered an item of found property in its storage facility, and a quick search reveals the owner's identity. Which of the following may be true?
    I. The law enforcement agency is not required to notify the owner.
    II. The owner usually has 90 days after the receipt of the property by the agency to prove his ownership and reclaim the property.

III. The item has become the property of the law enforcement agency.
IV. The agency is authorized to require payment by the owner of a reasonable charge to defray the cost of storage and care of the property.

A. I and II
B. I, II and III
C. II and IV
D. I, II, III and IV

KEY (CORRECT ANSWERS)

1. D
2. D
3. A
4. A
5. B

6. B
7. B
8. A
9. D
10. C

11. B
12. C
13. D
14. B
15. A

16. B
17. C
18. B
19. D
20. A

21. C
22. C
23. D
24. D
25. C

EXAMINATION SECTION

TEST 1

DIRECTIONS: Each question or incomplete statement is followed by several suggested answers or completions. Select the one that BEST answers the question or completes the statement. *PRINT THE LETTER OF THE CORRECT ANSWER IN THE SPACE AT THE RIGHT.*

Questions 1-6.

DIRECTIONS: Questions 1 through 6 are to be answered SOLELY on the basis of the numbered boxes on the Arrest Report and paragraph below.

ARREST REPORT

1. Arrest Number	2. Precinct of Arrest	3. Date/Time of Arrest	4. Defendant's Name		5. Defendant's Address
6. Defendant's Date of Birth	7. Sex	8. Race	9. Height	10. Weight	11. Location of Arrest	12. Date and Time of Occurrence
13. Location of Occurrence	14. Complaint Number	15. Victim's Name		16. Victim's Address	17. Victim's Date of Birth
18. Precinct of Complaint	19. Arresting Officer's Name	20. Shield Number		21. Assigned Unit Precinct	2. Date of Complaint

   On Friday, December 13 at 11:45 P.M., while leaving a store at 235 Spring Street, Grace O'Connell, a white female, 5'2" 130 lbs., was approached by a white male, 5'11", 200 lbs., who demanded her money and jewelry. As the man ran and turned down River Street, Police Officer William James, Shield Number 31724, assigned to the 14th Precinct, gave chase and apprehended him in front of 523 River Street. The prisoner, Gerald Grande, who resides at 17 Water Street, was arrested at 12:05 A.M., was charged with robbery, and taken to the 13th Precinct, where he was assigned Arrest Number 53048. Miss O'Connell, who resides at 275 Spring St., was given Complaint Number 822460.

1. On the basis of the Arrest Report and the above paragraph, the CORRECT entry for Box Number 3 should be
   A. 11:45 P.M., 12/13
   B. 11:45 P.M., 12/14
   C. 12:05 A.M., 12/13
   D. 12:05 A.M., 12/14

   1.____

2. On the basis of the Arrest Report and the above paragraph, the CORRECT entry for Box Number 21 should be
   A. 12th Precinct
   B. 14th Precinct
   C. Mounted Unit
   D. 32nd Precinct

   2.____

3. On the basis of the Arrest Report and the above paragraph, the CORRECT entry for Box Number 11 should be
   A. 235 Spring St. B. 523 River St.
   C. 275 Spring St. D. 17 Water St.

3._____

4. On the basis of the Arrest Report and the above paragraph, the CORRECT entry for Box Number 2 should be
   A. 13th Precinct B. 14th Precinct
   C. Mounted Unit D. 32nd Precinct

4._____

5. On the basis of the Arrest Report and the above paragraph, the CORRECT entry for Box Number 13 should be
   A. 523 River St. B. 17 Water St.
   C. 275 Spring St. D. 235 Spring St.

5._____

6. On the basis of the Arrest Report and the above paragraph, the CORRECT entry for Box Number 14 should be
   A. 53048 B. 31724 C. 12/13 D. 82460

6._____

Questions 7-10.

DIRECTIONS: Questions 7 through 10 are to be answered SOLELY on the basis of the following information.

You are required to file various documents in file drawers which are labeled according to the following pattern:

DOCUMENTS

MEMOS		LETTERS		REPORTS		INQUIRIES	
File	Subject	File	Subject	File	Subject	File	Subject
84PM1	(A-L)	84PC1	(A-L)	84PR1	(A-L)	84PQ1	(A-L)
84PM2	(M-Z)	84PC2	(M-Z)	84PR2	(M-Z)	84PQ2	(M-Z)

7. A letter dealing with a burglary should be filed in the drawer labeled
   A. 84PM1 B. 84PC1 C. 84PR1 D. 84PQ2

7._____

8. A report on *Statistics* should be found in the drawer labeled
   A. 84PM1 B. 84PC2 C. 84PR2 D. 84PQ2

8._____

9. An inquiry is received about parade permit procedures. It should be filed in the drawer labeled
   A. 84PM2 B. 84PC1 C. 84PR1 D. 84PQ2

9._____

10. A police officer has a question about a robbery report you filed. You should pull this file from the drawer labeled
    A. 84PM1 B. 84PM2 C. 84PR1 D. 84PR2

10._____

Questions 11-18.

DIRECTIONS: Questions 11 through 18 are to be answered SOLELY on the basis of the following information.

Below are listed the code number, name, and area of investigation of six detective units. Each question describes a crime.
For each question, choose the option (A, B, C, or D) which contains the code number for the detective unit responsible for handling that crime.

DETECTIVE UNITS

Unit Code No.	Unit Name	Unit's Area of Investigation
01	Senior Citizens Unit	All robberies of senior citizens 65 years or older
02	Major Case Unit	Any bank robbery; a commercial robbery where value of goods or money stolen is over $25,000
03	Robbery Unit	Any commercial, non-bank robbery where the value of the stolen goods or money is $25,000 or less; robberies of individuals under 65 years of age
04	Fraud and Larceny Unit	Confidence games and pickpockets
05	Special Investigations Unit	Burglaries of premises where the value of goods removed or monies taken is $15,000 or less
06	Burglary Unit	Burglaries of premises where the value of goods removed or monies taken is over $15,000

11. Mrs. Green calls the precinct and reports that her apartment was burglarized while she was on vacation and that precious jewelry and silverware, valued at $27,000, were taken.
    To which unit code number should her complaint be referred?
    A. 05   B. 02   C. 03   D. 06

12. Sylvia Bailey, Manager of the Building and Loan Savings Bank, reports that a man handed one of her tellers a note stating, *This is a robbery*. He had a gun and demanded money. The teller gave the man $500 in small bills, and the man then left.
    To which unit code should the complaint be referred?
    A. 02   B. 06   C. 03   D. 05

13. Mrs. Miniver, a 67-year-old widow, states that she was beaten and robbed by two men in the elevator of her apartment building.
    To which unit code number should the complaint be referred?
    A. 06   B. 01   C. 03   D. 02

13._____

14. Mr. Whipple, Manager of T.V.A. Supermarket, reports that during the night someone entered the store and removed merchandise valued at $12,500.
    To which unit code number should the complaint be referred?
    A. 05   B. 03   C. 06   D. 02

14._____

15. Mr. Gold, owner of Gold's Jewelry Exchange, reports that two men, armed with shotguns, robbed his store and removed money and jewelry valued at $28,000.
    To which unit code number should the complaint be referred?
    A. 05   B. 03   C. 06   D. 02

15._____

16. Mr. Watson, a 62-year-old man, was walking in Central Park when he was approached by a man with a knife and was robbed of $72.
    To which unit code number should the complaint be referred?
    A. 01   B. 06   C. 03   D. 02

16._____

17. The Ace Jewelry Manufacturing Company was broken into over the weekend when the building was closed. The owner stated that $35,000 in gold, silver, diamonds, and jewelry were taken.
    To which unit code number should the complaint be referred?
    A. 02   B. 03   C. 06   D. 05

17._____

18. Mrs. Vargas, 62, reports that she gave Mr. Greene of the Starlite Realty Corporation $1,000 to locate a new apartment for her family. A week went by, and she never heard from Mr. Greene. She called the Starlite Realty Corporation, and they informed her that Mr. Greene never worked for Starlite Realty Corporation and that they have no record of the $1,000 deposit of Mrs. Vargas.
    To which unit code number should the complaint be referred?
    A. 04   B. 03   C. 01   D. 05

18._____

Questions 19-24.

DIRECTIONS: Questions 19 through 24 consist of sentences which contain examples of correct or incorrect English usage. Examine each sentence with reference to grammar, spelling, punctuation, and capitalization. Choose one of the following options that would be BEST for correct English usage:
  A. The sentence is correct.
  B. There is one mistake.
  C. There are two mistakes.
  D. There are three mistakes.

19. Mrs. Fitzgerald came to the 59th Precinct to retreive her property which were stolen earlier in the week.

19._____

5 (#1)

20. The two officer's responded to the call, only to find that the perpatrator and the   20.____
    victim have left the scene.

21. Mr. Coleman called the 61st Precinct to report that, upon arriving at his store,   21.____
    he discovered that there was a large hole in the wall and that three boxes of
    radios were missing

22. The Administrative Leiutenant of the 62nd Precinct held a meeting which was   22.____
    attended by all the civilians, assigned to the Precinct.

23. Three days after the robbery occured the detective apprahended two   23.____
    suspects and recovered the stolen items.

24. The Community Affairs Officer of the 64th Precinct is the liaison between   24.____
    the Precinct and the community; he works closely with various community
    organizations, and elected officials.

Questions 25-32.

DIRECTIONS: Questions 25 through 32 are to be answered on the basis of the following
paragraph, which contains some deliberate errors in spelling and/or grammar
and/or punctuation. Each line of the paragraph is preceded by a number.
There are 9 lines and 9 numbers.

Line No.	Paragraph Line
1	The protection of life and property are, one of
2	the oldest and most important functions of a city.
3	New York city has its own full-time police Agency.
4	The police Department has the power an it shall
5	be there duty to preserve the Public piece,
6	prevent crime detect and arrest offenders, suppress
7	riots, protect the rites of persons and property, etc.
8	The maintainance of sound relations with the community they
9	serve is an important function of law enforcement officers.

25. How many errors are contained in line one?   25.____
    A. One   B. Two   C. Three   D. None

26. How many errors are contained in line two?   26.____
    A. One   B. Two   C. Three   D. None

27. How many errors are contained in line three?   27.____
    A. One   B. Two   C. Three   D. None

28. How many errors are contained in line four?   28.____
    A. One   B. Two   C. Three   D. None

29. How many errors are contained in line five? 29._____
    A. One   B. Two   C. Three   D. None

30. How many errors are contained in line six? 30._____
    A. One   B. Two   C. Three   D. None

31. How many errors are contained in line seven? 31._____
    A. One   B. Two   C. Three   D. None

32. How many errors are contained in line eight? 32._____
    A. One   B. Two   C. Three   D. None

Questions 33-40.

DIRECTIONS: Questions 33 through 40 are to be answered on the basis of the material contained in the INDEX OF CRIME IN CENTRAL CITY, U.S.A. 2011-2020 appearing below. Certain information is various columns is deliberately left blank.
The correct answer (A, B, C, or D) to these questions requires you to make computations that will enable you to fill in the blanks correctly.

	INDEX OF CRIME IN CENTRAL CITY, U.S.A., 2011-2020									
	Crime Index Total	Violent Crime[1]	Property Crime[2]	Murder	Forcible Rape	Robbery	Aggravated Assault	Burglary	Larceny Theft	Motor Vehicle Theft
2011	8,717	875		19	51	385	420	2,565	4,347	930
2012	10,252	974	9278	20	55	443	456		5,262	977
2013	11,256	1,026	10,230	20		465	485	3,253	5,977	1,000
2014	11,304	986		18	58	420	490	3,089	6,270	959
2015	10,935	1,009	9,926	19	63	405	522	3,053	5,605	968
2016	11,140	1,061	10,079	19	67	417	558	3,104	5,983	992
2017	12,152	1,178	10,974	23	75	466	614	3,299	6,578	1,097
2018	13,294	1,308	11,986	23	83		654	3,759	7,113	1,114
2019	13,289	1,321	11,968	22	82	574	643	3,740	7,154	1,074
2020	12,856	1,285	11,571	22	77	536	650	3,415	7,108	1,048

33. What was the TOTAL number of Property Crimes in 2011? 33._____
    A. 9,740   B. 10,252   C. 16,559   D. 7,842

34. What was the TOTAL number of Burglaries for 2012? 34._____
    A. 2,062   B. 3,039   C. 3,259   D. 4,001

35. In 2020, the total number of Aggravated Assaults was MOST NEARLY what percent of the total number of Violent Crimes for that year? 35._____
    A. 49.1   B. 46.3   C. 50.6   D. 41.7

36. In 2015, Property Crime was MOST NEARLY what percent of the Crime Index Total? 36._____
    A. 90.8   B. 9.3   C. 10.1   D. 89.9

37. What was the TOTAL number of Property Crimes for 2014? 37.____
    A. 10,318   B. 11,304   C. 98   D. 10,808

38. What was the TOTAL number of Robberies for 2018? 38.____
    A. 654   B. 571   C. 548   D. 1,202

39. Robbery made up what percent of the TOTAL number of Violent Crimes for 2020? 39.____
    A. 68.8%   B. 4.1%   C. 21.9%   D. 41.7%

40. What was the TOTAL number of Forcible Rapes for 2013? 40.____
    A. 47   B. 56   C. 55   D. 101

KEY (CORRECT ANSWERS)

1.	D	11.	D	21.	A	31.	A
2.	B	12.	A	22.	C	32.	A
3.	B	13.	B	23.	C	33.	D
4.	A	14.	A	24.	B	34.	B
5.	D	15.	D	25.	C	35.	C
6.	D	16.	C	26.	D	36.	A
7.	B	17.	C	27.	C	37.	A
8.	C	18.	A	28.	B	38.	C
9.	D	19.	C	29.	C	39.	D
10.	D	20.	D	30.	B	40.	B

TEST 2

DIRECTIONS: Each question or incomplete statement is followed by several suggested answers or completions. Select the one that BEST answers the question or completes the statement. *PRINT THE LETTER OF THE CORRECT ANSWER IN THE SPACE AT THE RIGHT.*

Questions 1-8.

DIRECTIONS: Each of Questions 1 through 8 consists of three lines of code letters and numbers. The numbers on each line should correspond to the code letters on the same line in accordance with the table below.

Code Letter	X	B	L	T	V	M	P	F	J	S
Corresponding Number	0	1	2	3	4	5	6	7	8	9

On some of the lines, an error exists in the coding. Compare the letters and numbers in each question carefully. If you find an error or errors on:
Only <u>one</u> of the lines in the question, mark your answer A;
Any <u>two</u> of the lines in the question, mark your answer B;
All <u>three</u> lines in the question, mark your answer C;
<u>None</u> of the lines in the question, mark your answer D.

SAMPLE QUESTION: MSXVLPT—5904263
SBFJLTP—9178246
XVMBTPF—8451367

In the above sample, the first line is correct since each code letter listed has the correct corresponding number. On the second line, an error exists because code letter T should have number 3 instead of number 4. On the third line, an error exists because the code letter X should have the number 0 instead of the number 8. Since there are errors on two of the three lines, the correct answer is B.

1. VFSTPLM—4793625
   SBXFLTP—9017236
   BT[JFSV—1358794   1.____

2. TSLFVPJ—3927468
   JLFTVXS—8273409
   MVSXBFL—5490172   2.____

3. XFTJSVT—0739843
   VFMTFLB—4753721
   LTFJSFM—2378985   3.____

4. SJMSJVL—9859742
   VFBXMPF—3710568
   PFPXLBS—7670219   4.____

5. MFPXVFP—5764076
    PTFJBLX—6378120
    VXSVSTB—4094931

    5.____

6. BXFPVJT—1076483
    STFMVLT—9375423
    TXPBTTM—3061335

    6.____

7. VLSBLVP—4290246
    FPSFBMV—7679154
    XTMXMLL—0730522

    7.____

8. JFVPMTJ—8746538
    TFPMXBL—3765012
    TJSFMFX—4987570

    8.____

Questions 9-18.

DIRECTIONS: Questions 9 through 18 each consists of two columns, each containing four lines of names, numbers and/or addresses. For each question, compare the lines in Column I with the lines in Column II to see if they match exactly, and mark your answer (A, B, C, or D) according to the following instructions:
A. all four lines match exactly
B. only three lines match exactly
C. only two lines match exactly
D. only one line matches exactly

9. (1) Earl Hodgson   Earl Hodgson
    (2) 1409870   1408970
    (3) Shore Ave.   Schore Ave.
    (4) Macon Rd.   Macon Rd.

    9.____

10. (1) 9671485   9671485
    (2) 470 Astor Court   470 Astor Court
    (3) Halprin, Phillip   Halperin, Phillip
    (4) Frank D. Poliseo   Frank D. Poliseo

    10.____

11. (1) Tandem Associates   Tandom Associates
    (2) 144-17 Northern Blvd. 144-17 Northern Blvd.
    (3) Alberta Forchi   Albert Forchi
    (4) Kings Park, NY 10751 Kings Point, NY 10751

    11.____

12. (1) Bertha C. McCormack Bertha C. McCormack
    (2) Clayton, MO   Clayton, MO
    (3) 976-4242   976-4242
    (4) New City, NY 10951 New City, NY 10951

    12.____

13.	(1) George C. Morill	George C. Morrill		13.____
	(2) Columbia, SC 29201	Columbia, SD 29201		
	(3) Louis Ingham	Louis Ingham		
	(4) 3406 Forest Ave.	3406 Forest Ave.		

13. (1) George C. Morill George C. Morrill 13.____
  (2) Columbia, SC 29201 Columbia, SD 29201
  (3) Louis Ingham Louis Ingham
  (4) 3406 Forest Ave. 3406 Forest Ave.

14. (1) 506 S. Elliott Pl. 506 S. Elliott Pl. 14.____
  (2) Herbert Hall Hurbert Hall
  (3) 4712 Rockaway Pkway 4712 Rockaway Pkway
  (4) 169 E. 7 St. 169 E. 7 St.

15. (1) 345 Park Ave. 345 Park Pl. 15.____
  (2) Colman Oven Corp. Coleman Oven Corp.
  (3) Robert Conte Robert Conti
  (4) 6179846 6179846

16. (1) Grigori Schierber Grigori Schierber 16.____
  (2) Des Moines, Iowa Des Moines, Iowa
  (3) Gouverneur Hospital Gouverneur Hospital
  (4) 91-35 Cresskill Pl. 91-35 Cresskill Pl.

17. (1) Jeffery Janssen Jeffrey Janssen 17.____
  (2) 8041071 8041071
  (3) 40 Rockefeller Plaza 40 Rockafeller Plaza
  (4) 407 6 St. 406 7 St.

18. (1) 5971996 5871996 18.____
  (2) 3113 Knickerbocker Ave. 3113 Knickerbocker Ave.
  (3) 8434 Boston Post Rd. 8424 Boston Post Rd.
  (4) Penn Station Penn Station

Questions 19-22.

DIRECTIONS: Questions 19 through 22 are to be answered by looking at the 4 groups of names and addresses listed below (I, II, III, and IV) and then finding out the number of groups that have their corresponding numbered lines exactly the same.

   Group I   Group II
Line 1 Ingersoll Public Library   Ingersoil Public Library
Line 2 Reference and Research Dept. Reference and Research Dept.
Line 3 95-12 238 St.   95-12 238 St.
Line 4 East Elmhurst, N.Y. 11357   East Elmhurst, N.Y. 11357

   Group III   Group IV
Line 1 Ingersoll Public Library   Ingersoll Pobblic Library
Line 2 Reference and Research Dept. Referance and Research Dept.
Line 3 92-15 283 St.   95-12 283 St.
Line 4 East Elmhurst, N.Y. 11357   East Elmhurst, N.Y. 1357

4 (#2)

19. In how many groups is line one exactly the same? 19.____
    A. Two   B. Three   C. Four   D. None

20. In how many groups is line two exactly the same? 20.____
    A. Two   B. Three   C. Four   D. None

21. In how many groups is line three exactly the same? 20.____
    A. Two   B. Three   C. Four   D. None

22. In how many groups is line four exactly the same? 22.____
    A. Two   B. Three   C. Four   E. None

Questions 23-26.

DIRECTIONS: Questions 23 through 26 are to be answered by looking at the 4 groups of names and addresses listed below (I, II, III, and IV) and then finding out the number of groups that have their corresponding numbered lines exactly the same.

Group I
Line 1 Richmond General Hospital
Line 2 Geriatric Clinic
Line 3 3975 Paerdegat St.
Line 4 Loudonville, New York 11538

Group II
Richman General Hospital
Geriatric Clinic
3975 Peardegat St.
Londonville, New York 11538

Group III
Line 1 Richmond General Hospital
Line 2 Geriatric Clinic
Line 3 3795 Paerdegat St.
Line 4 Loudonville, New York 11358

Group IV
Richmend General Hospital
Geriatric Clinic
3975 Paerdegat St.
Loudonville, New York 11538

23. In how many groups is line one exactly the same? 23.____
    A. Two   B. Three   C. Four   D. None

24. In how many groups is line two exactly the same? 24.____
    A. Two   B. Three   C. Four   D. None

25. In how many groups is line three exactly the same? 25.____
    A. Two   B. Three   C. Four   D. None

26. In how many groups is line four exactly the same? 26.____
    A. Two   B. Three   C. Four   D. None

Questions 27-34.

DIRECTIONS: Each of Questions 27 through 34 consists of four or six numbered names. For each question, choose the option (A, B, C, or D) which indicates the order in which the names should be filed in accordance with the following file instructions:

5 (#2)

- File alphabetically according to last name, then first name, then middle initial.
- File according to each successive letter within a name.
- When comparing two names where the letters in the longer name are identical with the corresponding letters in the shorter name, the shorter name is filed first.
- When the last names are the same, initials are always filed before names beginning with the same letter.

27. I.   Ralph Robinson
     II. Alfred Ross
     III. Luis Robles
     IV. James Roberts
     The CORRECT filing sequence for the above names should be
     A. IV, II, I, III   B. I, IV, III, II   C. III, IV, I, II   D. IV, I, III, II

28. I.   Irwin Goodwin
     II. Inez Gonzalez
     III. Irene Goodman
     IV. Ira S. Goodwin
     V.   Ruth I. Goldstein
     VI. M.B. Goodman
     The CORRECT filing sequence for the above names should be
     A. V, II, I, IV, III, VI   B. V, II, VI, III, IV, I
     C. V, II, III, VI, IV, I   D. V, II, III, VI, I, IV

29. I.   George Allan
     II. Gregory Allen
     III. Gary Allen
     IV. George Allen
     The CORRECT filing sequence for the above names should be
     A. IV, III, I, II   B. I, IV, II, III   C. III, IV, I, II   D. I, III, IV, II

30. I.   Simon Kauffman
     II. Leo Kauffman
     III. Robert Kaufmann
     IV. Paul Kauffman
     The CORRECT filing sequence for the above names should be
     A. I, IV, II, III   B. II, IV, I, III   C. III, II, IV, I   D. I, II, III, IV

31. I.   Roberta Williams
     II. Robin Wilson
     III. Roberta Wilson
     IV. Robin Williams
     The CORRECT filing sequence for the above names should be
     A. III, II, IV, I   B. I, IV, III, II   C. I, II, III, IV   D. III, I, II, IV

32.
I. Lawrence Shultz
II. Albert Schultz
III. Theodore Schwartz
IV. Thomas Schwarz
V. Alvin Schultz
VI. Leonard Shultz

The CORRECT filing sequence for the above names should be
A. II, V, III, IV, I, VI
B. IV, III, V, I, II, VI
C. II, V, I, VI, III, IV
D. I, VI, II, V, III, IV

33.
I. McArdle
II. Mayer
III. Maletz
IV. McNiff
V. Meyer
VI. MacMahon

The CORRECT filing sequence for the above names should be
A. I, IV, VI, III, II, V
B. II, I, IV, VI, III, V
C. VI, III, II, I, IV, V
D. VI, III, II, V, I, IV

34.
I. Jack E. Johnson
II. R.H. Jackson
III. Bertha Jackson
IV. J.T. Johnson
V. Ann Johns
VI. John Jacobs

The CORRECT filing sequence for the above names should be
A. II, III, VI, V, IV, I
B. III, II, VI, V, IV, I
C. VI, II, III, I, V, IV
D. III, II, VI, IV, V, I

Questions 35-40.

DIRECTIONS: Questions 35 through 40 are to be answered SOLELY on the basis of the following passage.

An aide assigned to the Complaint Room must be familiar with the various forms used by that office. Some of these forms and their uses are:

Complaint Report: Used to record information on or information about crimes reported to the Police Department.
Complaint Report Follow-Up: Used to record additional information after the initial complaint report has been filed
Aided Card: Used to record information pertaining to sick and injured persons aided by the police.
Accident Report: Used to record information on or information about injuries and/or property damage involving motorized vehicles.
Property Vouch: Used to record information on or information about property which comes into possession of the Police Department. (Motorized vehicles are not included.)

Auto Voucher: Used to record information on or information about a motorized vehicle which comes into possession of the Police Department.

35. Mr. Brown walks into the police precinct and informs the Administrative Aide that, while he was at work, someone broke into his apartment and removed property belonging to him. He does not know everything that was taken, but he wants to make a report now and will make a list of what was taken and bring it in later.
   According to the above passage, the CORRECT form to use in this situation should be the
   A. Property Voucher
   B. Complaint Report
   C. Complaint Report Follow-Up
   D. Aided Card

36. Mrs. Wilson telephones the precinct and informs the Administrative Aide she wishes to report additional property which was taken from her apartment. The Administrative Aide finds a Complaint Report had been previously filed for Mrs. Wilson.
   According to the above passage, the CORRECT form to use in this situation should be the
   A. Property Voucher
   B. Complaint Report
   C. Complaint Report Follow-Up
   D. Aided Card

37. Police Officer Jones walks into the Complaint Room and informs the Administrative Aide that, while he was on patrol, he observed a woman fall to the sidewalk and remain there, apparently hurt. He comforted the injured woman and called for an ambulance, which came and brought the woman to the hospital.
   According to the above passage, the CORRECT form on which to record this information should be the
   A. Accident Report
   B. Complaint Report
   C. Complaint Report Follow-Up
   D. Aided Card

38. Police Officer Smith informed the Administrative Aide assigned to the Complaint Room that Mr. Green, while crossing the street, was struck by a motorcycle and had to be taken to the hospital.
   According to the above passage, the facts regarding this incident should be recorded on which one of the following forms?
   A. Accident Report
   B. Complaint Report
   C. Complaint Report Follow-Up
   D. Aided Card

39. Police Officer Williams reports to the Administrative Aide assigned to the Complaint Room that he and his partner, Police Officer Murphy, found an auto which was reported stolen and had the auto towed into the police garage.
   Of the following forms listed in the above passage, which is the CORRECT one to use to record this information?
   A. Property Voucher
   B. Auto Voucher
   C. Complaint Report Follow-Up
   D. Complaint Report

40. Administrative Aide Lopez has been assigned to the Complaint Room. During her tour of duty, a person who does not identify herself hands Ms. Lopez a purse. The person states that she found the purse on the street. She then leaves the station house.
   According to the information in the above passage, which is the CORRECT form to fill out to record the incident?
   A. Property Voucher
   B. Auto Voucher
   C. Complaint Report Follow-Up
   D. Complaint Report

KEY (CORRECT ANSWERS)

1.	B	11.	D	21.	A	31.	B
2.	D	12.	A	22.	C	32.	A
3.	B	13.	C	23.	A	33.	C
4.	C	14.	B	24.	C	34.	B
5.	A	15.	D	25.	A	35.	B
6.	D	16.	A	26.	A	36.	C
7.	C	17.	D	27.	D	37.	D
8.	A	18.	C	28.	C	38.	A
9.	C	19.	A	29.	D	39.	B
10.	B	20.	B	30.	B	40.	A

EVALUATING INFORMATION AND EVIDENCE
SAMPLE QUESTIONS

These questions test for the ability to evaluate and draw conclusions from information and evidence. Each question consists of a set of facts and a conclusion based on the facts. You must decide if the conclusion is warranted by the facts.

TEST TASK: You will be given a set of FACTS and a CONCLUSION based on the facts. The conclusion is derived from these facts only—NOT on what you may happen to know about the subject discussed. Each question has three possible answers. You must then select the correct answer in the following manner:

>Select A if the statements prove that the conclusion is TRUE.
>Select B if the statements prove that the conclusion is FALSE.
>Select C if the statements are INADEQUATE to prove the conclusion EITHER TRUE OR FALSE.

SAMPLE QUESTION #1

FACTS: All uniforms are cleaned by the Conroy Company. Blue uniforms are cleaned on Mondays or Fridays; green or brown uniforms are cleaned on Wednesdays. Alan and Jean have blue uniforms, Gary has green uniforms, and Ryan has brown uniforms.

CONCLUSION: Jean's uniforms are cleaned on Wednesdays.
The correct answer to this sample question is B.

SOLUTION: The last sentence of the FACTS says that Jean has blue uniforms. The second sentence of the FACTS says that blue uniforms are cleaned on Monday or Friday. The CONCLUSION says Jean's uniforms are cleaned on Wednesday. Wednesday is neither Monday nor Friday. Therefore, the conclusion must be FALSE (choice B).

SAMPLE QUESTION #2

FACTS: If Beth works overtime, the assignment will be completed. If the assignment is completed, then all unit employees will receive a bonus. Beth works overtime.

CONCLUSION: A bonus will be given to all employees in the unit.
The correct answer to this sample question is A.

SOLUTION: The CONCLUSION follows necessarily from the FACTS. Beth works overtime. The assignment is completed. Therefore, all unit employees will receive a bonus.

SAMPLE QUESTION #3

FACTS: Bill is older than Wanda. Edna is older than Bill. Sarah is twice as old as Wanda.

CONCLUSION: Sarah is older than Edna.
The correct answer to this Sample Question #3 is C.

SOLUTION: We know from the facts that both Sarah and Edna are older than Wanda. We do not have any other information about Sarah and Edna. Therefore, no conclusion about whether or not Sarah is older than Edna can be made.

EVALUATING INFORMATION AND EVIDENCE
EXAMINATION SECTION
TEST 1

DIRECTIONS: Each question or incomplete statement is followed by several suggested answers or completions. Select the one that BEST answers the question or completes the statement. *PRINT THE LETTER OF THE CORRECT ANSWER IN THE SPACE AT THE RIGHT.*

Questions 1-9.

DIRECTIONS: Questions 1 through 9 measure your ability to (1) determine whether statements from witnesses say essentially the same thing and (2) determine the evidence needed to make it reasonably certain that a particular conclusion is true.

1. Which of the following pairs of statements say essentially the same thing in two different ways?
   I. Some employees at the water department have fully vested pensions.
      At least one employee at the water department has a pension that is not fully vested.
   II. All swans are white birds.
       A bird that is not white is not a swan.
   The CORRECT answer is:
   A. I only   B. I and II   C. II only   D. Neither I nor II

   1.____

2. Which of the following pairs of statements say essentially the same thing in two different ways?
   I. If you live in Humboldt County, your property taxes are high.
      If your property taxes are high, you live in Humboldt County.
   II. All the Hutchinsons live in Lindsborg.
       At least some Hutchinsons do not live in Lindsborg.
   The CORRECT answer is;
   A. I only   B. I and II   C. II only   D. Neither I nor II

   2.____

3. Which of the following pairs of statements say essentially the same thing in two different ways?
   I. Although Spike is a friendly dog, he is also one of the most unpopular dogs on the block.
      Although Spike is one of the most unpopular dogs on the block, he is a friendly dog.
   II. Everyone in Precinct 19 is taller than Officer Banks.
       Nobody in Precinct 19 is shorter than Officer Banks.
   The CORRECT answer is:
   A. I only   B. I and II   C. II only   D. Neither I nor II

   3.____

4. Which of the following pairs of statements say essentially the same thing in two different ways?
   I. On Friday, every officer in Precinct 1 is assigned parking duty or crowd control, or both.
      If a Precinct 1 officer has been assigned neither parking duty nor crowd control, it is not Friday.
   II. Because the farmer mowed the hay fields today, his house will have mice tomorrow.
      Whenever the farmer mows his hay fields, his house has mice the next day.
   The CORRECT answer is:
   A. I only   B. I and II   C. II only   D. Neither I nor II

   4.____

5. Summary of Evidence Collected to Date:
   I. Fishing in the Little Pony River is against the law.
      Captain Rick caught an 8-inch trout and ate it for dinner.
   Prematurely Drawn Conclusion: Captain Rick broke the law.
   Which of the following pieces of evidence, if any, would make it reasonably certain that the conclusion drawn is true?
   A. Captain Rick caught his trout in the Little Pony River.
   B. There is no size limit on trout mentioned in the law.
   C. A trout is a species of fish.
   D. None of the above

   5.____

6. Summary of Evidence Collected to Date:
   I. Some of the doctors in the ICU have been sued for malpractice.
   II. Some of the doctors in the ICU are pediatricians.
   Prematurely Drawn Conclusion: Some of the pediatricians in the ICU have never been sued for malpractice.
   Which of the following pieces of evidence, if any, would make it reasonably certain that the conclusion drawn is true?
   A. The number of pediatricians in the ICU is the same as the number of doctors who have been sued for malpractice.
   B. The number of pediatricians in the ICU is smaller than the number of doctors who have been sued for malpractice.
   C. The number of ICU doctors who have been sued for malpractice is smaller than the number who are pediatricians.
   D. None of the above

   6.____

7. Summary of Evidence Collected to Date:
   I. Along Paseo Boulevard, there are five convenience stores.
   II. EZ-GO is east of Pop-a-Shop.
   III. Kwik-E-Mart is west of Bob's Market.
   IV. The Nightwatch is between EZ-GO and Kwik-E-Mart.
   Prematurely Drawn Conclusion: Pop-a-Shop is the westernmost convenience store on Paseo Boulevard.

   7.____

3 (#1)

Which of the following pieces of evidence, if any, would make it reasonably certain that the conclusion drawn is true?
   A. Bob's Market is the easternmost convenience store on Paseo.
   B. Kwik-E-Mart is the second store from the west.
   C. The Nightwatch is west of the EZ-GO.
   D. None of the above

8. Summary of Evidence Collected to Date: 8.____
Stark drove home from work at 70 miles an hour and wasn't breaking the law.
Prematurely Drawn Conclusion: Stark was either on an interstate highway or in the state of Montana.
Which of the following pieces of evidence, if any, would make it reasonably certain that the conclusion drawn is true?
   A. There are no interstate highways in Montana.
   B. Montana is the only state that allows a speed of 70 miles an hour on roads other than interstate highways.
   C. Most states don't allow speed of 70 miles an hour on state highways.
   D. None of the above

9. Summary of Evidence Collected to Date: 9.____
   I. Margaret, owner of MetroWoman magazine, signed a contract with each of her salespeople promising an automatic $200 bonus to any employee who sells more than 60 subscriptions in a calendar month.
   II. Lynn sold 82 subscriptions to MetroWoman in the month of December.
Prematurely Drawn Conclusion: Lynn received a $20 bonus.
Which of the following pieces of evidence, if any, would make it reasonably certain that the conclusion is true?
   A. Lynn is a salesperson.
   B. Lynn works for Margaret.
   C. Margaret offered only $200 regardless of the number of subscriptions sold.
   D. None of the above

Questions 10-14.

DIRECTIONS: Questions 10 through 14 refer to Map #3 and measure your ability to orient yourself within a given section of town, neighborhood or particular area. Each of the questions describes a starting point and a destination. Assume that you are driving a car in the area shown on the map accompanying the questions. Use the map as a basis for the shortest way to get from one point to another without breaking the law.
On the map, a street marked by arrows, or by arrows and the words "One Way," indicates one-way travel and should be assumed to be one-way for the entire length, even when there are breaks or jogs in the street. EXCEPTION: A street that does not have the same name over the full length.

4 (#1)

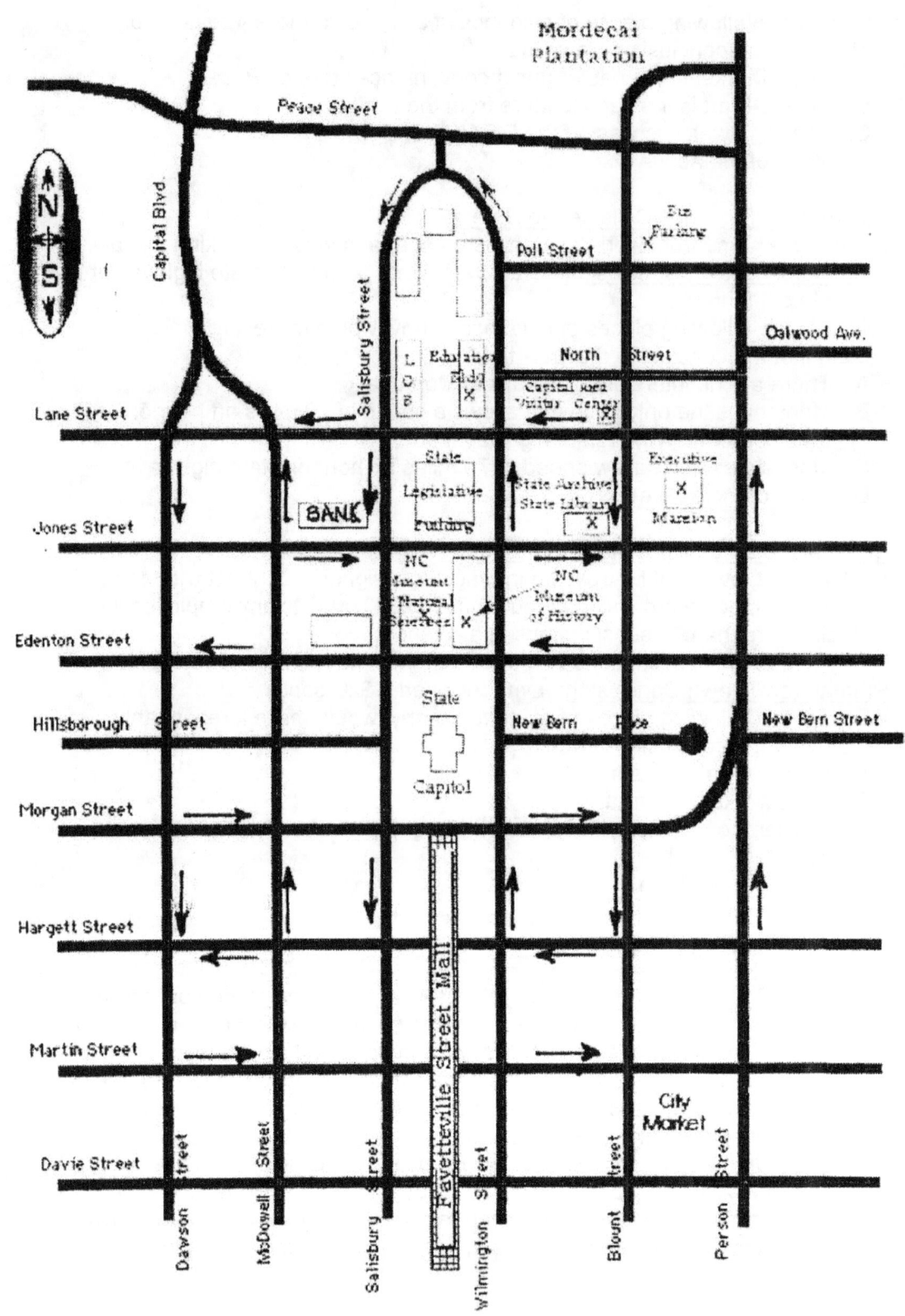

5 (#1)

10. The SHORTEST legal way from the south end of the Fayetteville Street Mall, at Davie Street, to the city of Raleigh Municipal Building is
    A. west on Davie, north on McDowell
    B. west on Davie, north on Dawson
    C. east on Davie, north on Wilmington, west on Morgan
    D. east on Davie, north on Wilmington, west on Hargett

10.____

11. The SHORTEST legal way from the City Market to the Education Building is
    A. north on Blount, west on North
    B. north on Person, west on Lane
    C. north on Blount, west on Lane
    D. west on Martin, north on Wilmington

11.____

12. The SHORTEST legal way from the Education Building to the State Capitol is
    A. south on Wilmington
    B. north on Wilmington, west on Peace, south on Capitol, bear west to go south on Dawson, and east on Morgan
    C. west on Lane, south on Salisbury
    D. each on North, south on Blount, west on Edenton

12.____

13. The SHORTEST legal way from the State Capitol to Peace College is
    A. north on Wilmington, jog north, east on Peace
    B. east on Morgan, north on Person, west on Peace
    C. west on Edenton, north on McDowell, north on Capitol Blvd., east on Peace
    D. east on Morgan, north on Blount, west on Peace

13.____

14. The SHORTEST legal way from the State Legislative Building to the City Market is
    A. south on Wilmington, east on Martin
    B. east on Jones, south on Blount
    C. south on Salisbury, east on Davie
    D. east on Lane, south on Blount

14.____

Questions 15-19.

DIRECTIONS: Questions 15 through 19 refer to Figure #3, on the following page, and measure your ability to understand written descriptions of events. Each question presents a description of an accident or event and asks you which of the following five drawings in Figure #3 BEST represents it.
In the drawings, the following symbols are used:
Moving vehicle ◊   Non-moving vehicle ♦
Pedestrian or bicyclist •
The path and direction of travel of a vehicle or pedestrian is indicated by a solid line.
The path and direction of travel of each vehicle or pedestrian directly involved in a collision from the point of impact is indicated by a dotted line.

6 (#1)

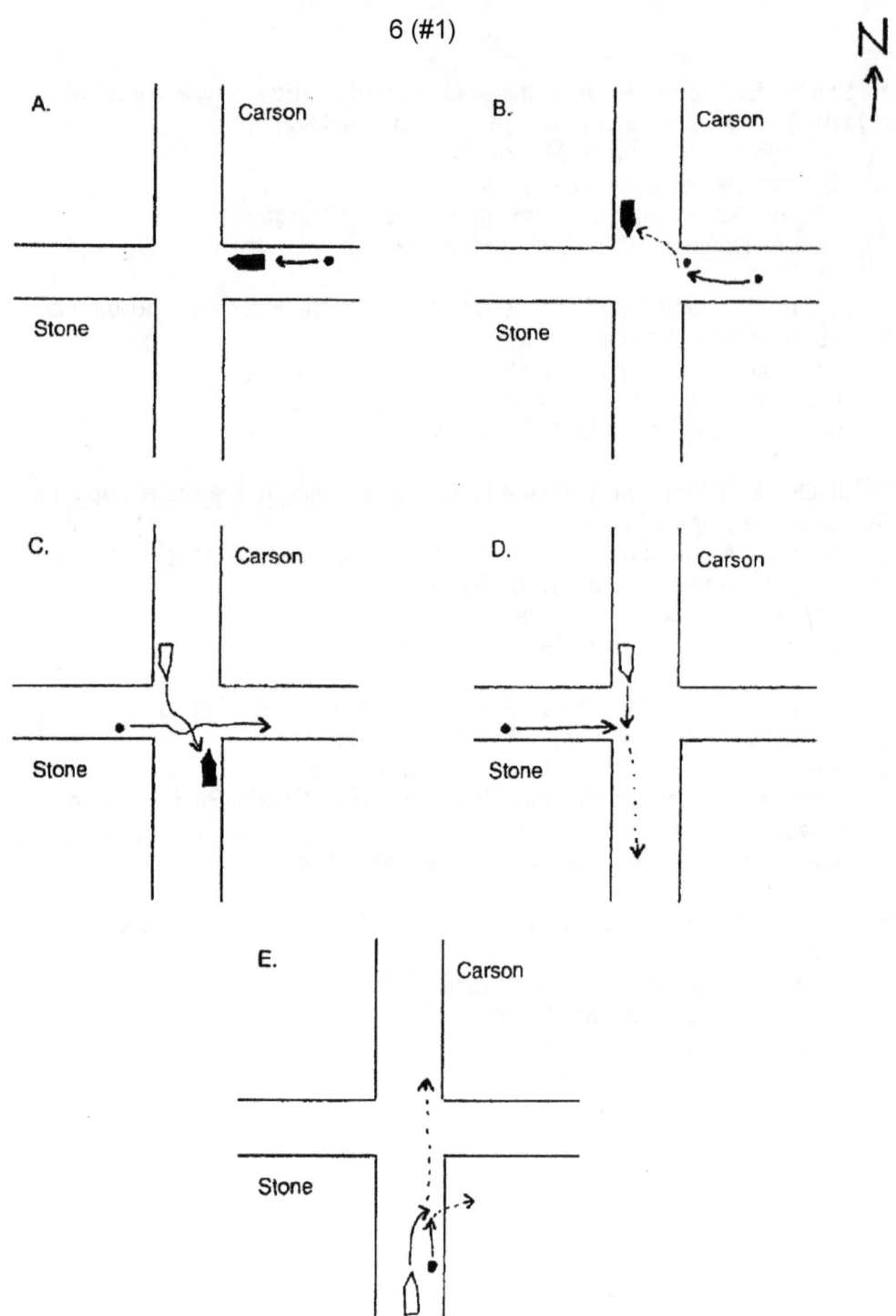

In the space at the right, print the letter of the drawing that BEST fit the descriptions written below.

15. A driver headed north on Carson veers to the right and strikes a bicyclist who is also headed north. The bicyclist is thrown from the road. The driver flees north on Carson.

15._____

16. A driver heading south on Carson runs the stop sign and barely misses colliding with an eastbound cyclist. The cyclist swerves to avoid the collision and continues traveling east. The driver swerves to avoid the collision and strikes a car parked in the northbound lane on Carson.

16._____

17. A bicyclist heading west on Stone collides with a pedestrian in the crosswalk, then veers through the intersection and collides with the front of a car parked in the southbound lane on Carson.

17._____

18. A driver traveling south on Carson runs over a bicyclist who has run the stop sign, and then flees south on Carson.

18._____

19. A bicyclist heading west on Stone collides with the rear of a car parked in the westbound lane.

19._____

Questions 20-22.

DIRECTIONS: In Questions 20 through 22, choose the word or phrase CLOSEST in meaning to the word or phrase printed in capital letters.

20. INSOLVENT
    A. bankrupt   B. vagrant   C. hazardous   D. illegal

20._____

21. TENANT
    A. laborer   B. occupant   C. owner   D. creditor

21._____

22. INFRACTION
    A. portion   B. violation   C. remark   D. detour

22._____

Questions 23-25.

DIRECTIONS: Questions 23 through 25 measure your ability to do fieldwork-related arithmetic. Each question presents a separate arithmetic problem for you to solve.

23. Officer Jones has served on the police force longer than Smith. Smith has served longer than Moore. Moore has served less time than Jones, and Park has served longer than Jones.
Which officer has served the LONGEST on the police force?
    A. Jones   B. Smith   C. Moore   D. Park

23._____

24. A car wash has raised the price of an outside-only wash from $4 to $5. The car wash applies the same percentage increase to its inside-and-out wash, which was $10.
What is the new cost of the inside-and-out wash?
    A. $8   B. $11   C. $12.50   D. $15

24._____

25. Ron and James, college students, make $10 an hour working at the restaurant. Ron works 13 hours a week and James works 20 hours a week. To make the same amount that Ron earns in a year, James would work about _____ weeks.

    A. 18   B. 27   C. 34   D. 45

25.____

KEY (CORRECT ANSWERS)

1.	C	11.	B
2.	D	12.	C
3.	B	13.	A
4.	B	14.	B
5.	A	15.	E
6.	D	16.	C
7.	B	17.	B
8.	B	18.	D
9.	B	19.	A
10.	A	20.	A

21. B
22. B
23. D
24. C
25. C

SOLUTIONS TO QUESTIONS 1-9

P implies Q = original statement

Not Q implies not P = contrapositive of the original statement. A statement and its contrapositive are logically equivalent.

Q implies P = converse of the original statement

Not P implies not Q = inverse of the original statement. The converse and inverse of an original statement are logically equivalent.

P implies Q = Not P or Q.

1. The CORRECT answer is C.
   Item I is wrong because "some employees" means "at least one employee" and possibly "all employees." If it is true that all employees have fully vested pensions, then the second statement is false. Item II is correct because the second statement is the contrapositive of the first statement.

2. The CORRECT answer is D.
   Item I is wrong because the converse of a statement does not necessarily follow from the original statement. Item II is wrong because statement I implies that there are no Hutchinson family members who live outside Lindsborg.

3. The CORRECT answer is B. Item I is correct because it is composed of the same two compound statements that are simply mentioned in a different order. Item II is correct because if each person is taller than Officer Banks, then there is no person in that precinct who can possibly be shorter than Officer Banks.

4. The CORRECT answer is B.
   Item I is correct because the second statement is the contrapositive of the first statement. Item II is correct because each statement indicates that mowing the hay fields on a particular day leads to the presence of mice the next day.

5. The CORRECT answer is A.
   If Captain Rick caught his trout in the Little Pony River, then we can conclude that he was fishing there. Since statement I says that fishing in the Little Pony Rive is against the law, we conclude that Captain Rick broke the law.

6. The CORRECT answer is D.
   The number of doctors in each group, whether the same or not, has no bearing on the conclusion. There is nothing in evidence to suggest that the group of doctors sued for malpractice overlaps with the group of doctors that are pediatricians.

7. The CORRECT answer is B.
   If we are given that Kwik-E-Mart is the second store from the west, then the order of stores from west to east, is Pop-a-Shop, Kwik-E-Mart, Nightwatch, EZ-GO, and Bob's Market.

8. The CORRECT answer is B.
We are given that Stark drove at 70 miles per hour and didn't break the law. If we also know that Montana is the only state that allows a speed of 70 miles per hour, then we can conclude that Stark must have been driving in Montana or else was driving on some interstate.

9. The CORRECT answer is B.
The only additional piece of information needed is that Lynn works for Margaret. This will guarantee that Lynn receives the promised $200 bonus.

TEST 2

DIRECTIONS: Each question or incomplete statement is followed by several suggested answers or completions. Select the one that BEST answers the question or completes the statement. *PRINT THE LETTER OF THE CORRECT ANSWER IN THE SPACE AT THE RIGHT.*

Questions 1-9.

DIRECTIONS: Questions 1 through 9 measure your ability to (1) determine whether statements from witnesses say essentially the same thing and (2) determine the evidence needed to make it reasonably certain that a particular conclusion is true.
To do well on this part of the test, you do NOT have to have a working knowledge of police procedures and techniques. Nor do you have to have any more familiarity with criminals and criminal behavior than that acquired from reading newspapers, listening to radio or watching TV. To do well in this part, you must read and reason carefully.

1. Which of the following pairs of statements say essentially the same thing in two different ways?
   I. All of the teachers at Slater Middle School are intelligent, but some are irrational thinkers.
      Although some teachers at Slater Middle School are irrational thinkers, all of them are intelligent.
   II. Nobody has no friends.
       Everybody has at least one friend.
   The CORRECT answer is:
   A. I only   B. I and II   C. II only   D. Neither I nor II

2. Which of the following pairs of statements say essentially the same thing in two different ways?
   I. Although bananas taste good to most people, they are also a healthy food.
      Bananas are a healthy food, but most people eat them because they taste good.
   II. If Dr. Jones is in, we should call at the office.
       Either Dr. Jones is in, or we should not call at the office.
   The CORRECT answer is:
   A. I only   B. I and II   C. II only   D. Neither I nor II

3 Which of the following pairs of statements say essentially the same thing in two different ways?
   I. Some millworker work two shifts.
      If someone works only one shift, he is probably not a millworker.
   II. If a letter carrier clocks in at nine, he can finish his route by the end of the day.
       If a letter carrier does not clock in at nine, he cannot finish his route by the end of the day.
   The CORRECT answer is:
   A. I only   B. I and II   C. II only   D. Neither I nor II

39

4. Which of the following pairs of statements say essentially the same thing in two different ways?
   I. If a member of the swim team attends every practice, he will compete in the next meet.
      Either a swim team member will compete in the next meet, or he did not attend every practice.
   II. All the engineers in the drafting department who wear glasses know how to use AutoCAD.
      If an engineer wears glasses, he will know how to use AutoCAD.
   The CORRECT answer is:
   A. I only   B. I and II   C. II only   D. Neither I nor II

5. Summary of Evidence Collected to Date:
   All of the parents who attend the weekly parenting seminars are high school graduates.
   Prematurely Drawn Conclusion: Some parents who attend the weekly parenting seminars have been convicted of child abuse.
   Which of the following pieces of evidence, if any, would make it reasonably certain that the conclusion drawn is true?
   A. Those convicted of child abuse are often high school graduates.
   B. Some high school graduates have been convicted of child abuse.
   C. There is no correlation between education level and the incidence of child abuse.
   D. None of the above

6. Summary of Evidence Collected to Date:
   I. Mr. Cantwell promised to vote for new school buses if he was reelected to the board.
   II. If the new school buses are approved by the school board, then Mr. Cantwell was not reelected to the board.
   Prematurely Drawn Conclusion: Approval of the new school buses was defeated in spite of Mr. Cantwell's vote.
   Which of the following pieces of evidence, if any, would make it reasonably certain that the conclusion drawn is true?
   A. Mr. Cantwell decided not to run for reelection.
   B. Mr. Cantwell was reelected to the board.
   C. Mr. Cantwell changed his mind and voted against the new buses.
   D. None of the above

7. Summary of Evidence Collected to Date:
   I. The station employs three detectives: Francis, Jackson, and Stern. One of the detectives is a lieutenant, one is a sergeant, and one is a major.
   II. Francis is not a lieutenant.
   Prematurely Drawn Conclusion: Jackson is a lieutenant.
   Which of the following pieces of evidence, if any, would make it reasonably certain that the conclusion drawn is true?
   A. Stern is not a sergeant.   B. Stern is a major.
   C. Francis is a major.   E. None of the above

8. Summary of Evidence Collected to Date:
   I. In the office building, every survival kit that contains a gas mask also contains anthrax vaccine.
   II. Some of the kits containing water purification tablets also contain anthrax vaccine.

   Prematurely Drawn Conclusion: If the survival kit near the typists' pool contains a gas mask, it does not contain water purification tablets.
   Which of the following pieces of evidence, if any, would make it reasonably certain that the conclusion drawn is true?
   A. Some survival kits contain all three items.
   B. The survival kit near the typists' pool contains anthrax vaccine.
   C. The survival kit near the typists' pool contains only two of these items.
   D. None of the above

9. Summary of Evidence Collected to Date:
   The shrink-wrap mechanism is designed to shut itself off if the heating coil temperature drops below 400 during the twin cycle.
   Prematurely Drawn Conclusion: If the machine was operating the twin cycle on Monday, it was not operating properly.
   Which of the following pieces of evidence, if any, would make it reasonably certain that the conclusion drawn is true?
   A. On Monday, the heating coil temperature reached 450.
   B. When the machine performs functions other than the twin cycle, the heating coil temperature sometimes drops below 400.
   C. The shrink-wrap mechanism did not shut itself off on Monday.
   D. None of the above

Questions 10-14.

DIRECTIONS: Questions 10 through 14 refer to Map #3 and measure your ability to orient yourself within a given section of town, neighborhood or particular area. Each of the questions describes a starting point and a destination. Assume that you are driving a car in the area shown on the map accompanying the questions. Use the map as a basis for the shortest way to get from one point to another without breaking the law.
On the map, a street marked by arrows, or by arrows and the words "One Way," indicates one-way travel and should be assumed to be one-way for the entire length, even when there are breaks or jogs in the street. EXCEPTION: A street that does not have the same name over the full length.

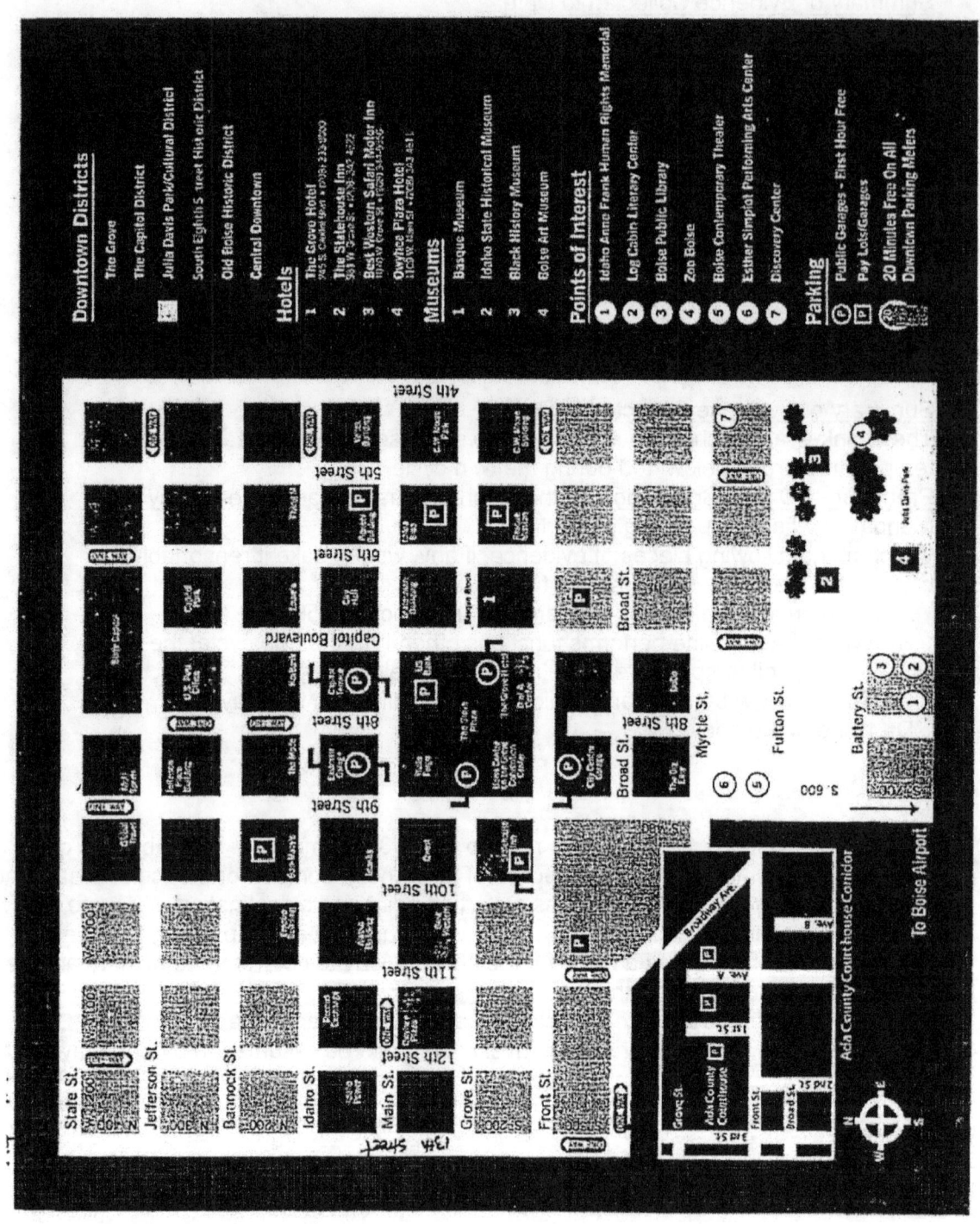

10. The SHORTEST legal way from the State Capitol to Idaho Power is
    A. south on Capitol Blvd., west on Main, north on 12th
    B. south on 8th, west on Main
    C. west on Jefferson, south on 12th
    D. south on Capitol Blvd., west on Front, north on 12th

11. The SHORTEST legal way from the Jefferson Place Building to the Statesman Building is   11._____
    A. east on Jefferson, south on Capitol Blvd.
    B. south on 8th, east on Main
    C. east on Jefferson, south on 4th, west on Main
    D. south on 9th, east on Main

12. The SHORTEST legal way from Julia Davis Park to Owyhee Plaza Hotel is   12._____
    A. north on 5th, west on Front, north on 11th
    B. north on 6th, west on Main
    C. west on Battery, north on 9th, west on Front, north on Main
    D. north on 5th, west on Front, north on 13th, east on Main

13. The SHORTEST legal way from the Big Easy to City Hall is   13._____
    A. north on 9th, east on Main
    B. east on Myrtle, north on Capitol Blvd.
    C. north on 9th, east on Idaho
    D. east on Myrtle, north on 6th

14. The SHORTEST legal way from the Boise Contemporary Theater to the Pioneer Building is   14._____
    A. north on 9th, east on Main
    B. north on 9th, east on Myrtle, north on 6th
    C. east on Fulton, north on Capitol Blvd., east on Main
    D. east on Fulton, north on 6th

Questions 15-19.

DIRECTIONS: Questions 15 through 19 refer to Figure #3, on the following page, and measure your ability to understand written descriptions of events. Each question presents a description of an accident or event and asks you which of the following five drawings in Figure #3 BEST represents it.
In the drawings, the following symbols are used:
Moving vehicle ⌂   Non-moving vehicle ♦
Pedestrian or bicyclist •
The path and direction of travel of a vehicle or pedestrian is indicated by a solid line.
The path and direction of travel of each vehicle or pedestrian directly involved in a collision from the point of impact is indicated by a dotted line.

In the space at the right, print the letter of the drawing that BEST fit the descriptions written below.

6 (#2)

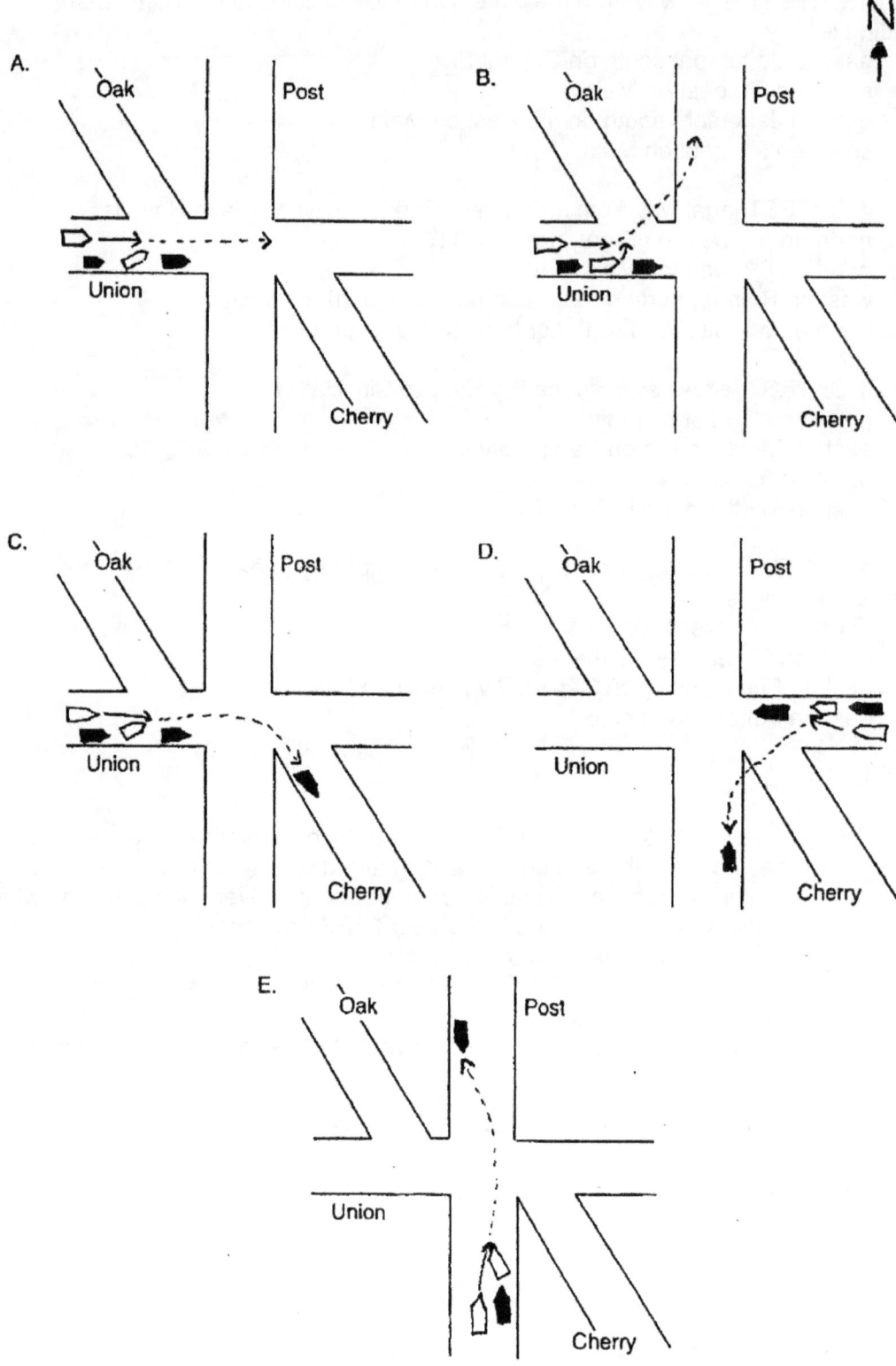

15. A driver headed east on Union strikes a car that is pulling out from between two parked cars, and then continues east.   15.____

16. A driver headed north on Post strikes a car that is pulling out from in front of a parked car, then veers into the oncoming lane and collides head-on with a car that is parked in the southbound lane of Post.   16.____

17. A driver headed east on Union strikes a car that is pulling out from two parked cars, travels through the intersection, and makes a sudden right turn onto Cherry, where he strikes a parked car in the rear.   17.____

18. A driver headed west on Union strikes a car that is pulling out from between two parked cars, and then swerves to the left. He cuts the corner and travels over the sidewalk at the intersection of Cherry and Post, and then strikes a car that is parked in the northbound lane on Post.   18.____

19. A driver headed east on Union strikes a car that is pulling out from between two parked cars, and then swerves to the left. He cuts the corner and travels over the sidewalk at the intersection of Oak and Post, and then flees north on Post.   19.____

Questions 20-22.

DIRECTIONS: In Questions 20 through 22, choose the word or phrase CLOSEST in meaning to the word or phrase printed in capital letters.

20. TITLE   20.____
    A. danger   B. ownership   C. description   D. treatise

21. REVOKE   21.____
    A. cancel   B. imagine   C. solicit   D. cause

22. BRIEF   22.____
    A. summary   B. ruling   C. plea   D. motion

Questions 23-25.

DIRECTIONS: Questions 23 through 25 measure your ability to do fieldwork-related arithmetic. Each question presents a separate arithmetic problem for you to solve.

23. An investigator plans to drive from his home to Los Angeles, a trip of 2,800 miles. His car has a 24-gallon tank and gets 18 miles to the gallon. If he starts out with a full tank of gasoline, what is the FEWEST number of stops he will have to make for gasoline to complete his trip to Los Angeles?   23.____
    A. 4   B. 5   C. 6   D. 7

24. A caseworker has 24 home visits to schedule for a week. She will visit three homes on Sunday, and on every day that follows she will visit one more home than she visited on the previous day.
At the end of the day on _____, the caseworker will have completed all of her home visits.
   A. Wednesday   B. Thursday   C. Friday   D. Saturday

24.____

25. Ms. Langhorn takes a cab from her house to the airport. The cab company charges $3.00 to start the meter and $.50 per mile after that. It's 15 miles from Ms. Langhorn's house to the airport.
How much will she have to pay for a cab?
   A. $10.50   B. $11.50   C. $14.00   D. $15.50

25.____

KEY (CORRECT ANSWERS)

1.	B		11.	D
2.	A		12.	A
3.	D		13.	B
4.	B		14.	C
5.	D		15.	A
6.	B		16.	E
7.	B		17.	C
8.	C		18.	D
9.	C		19.	B
10.	C		20.	B

21. A
22. A
23. C
24. B
25. A

SOLUTIONS TO QUESTIONS 1-9

P implies Q = original statement

Not Q implies not P = contrapositive of the original statement. A statement and its contrapositive are logically equivalent.

Q implies P = converse of the original statement

Not P implies not Q = inverse of the original statement. The converse and inverse of an original statement are logically equivalent.

P implies Q = Not P or Q.

1. The CORRECT answer is B.
   For Item I, the irrational thinking teachers at the Middle School belong the group of all Middle School teachers. Since all teachers at the Middle School are intelligent, this includes the subset of irrational thinkers. For item II, if no one person has no friends, this implies that each person must have at least one friend.

2. The CORRECT answer is A.
   In item I, both statements state that (a) bananas are healthy and (b) bananas are eaten mainly because they taste good. In item II, the second statement is not equivalent to the first statement. An equivalent statement to the first statement would be "Either Dr. Jones is not in or we should call at the office."

3. The CORRECT answer is D.
   In item I, given that a person works one shift, we cannot draw any conclusion about whether he/she is a millworker. It is possible that a millworker works one, two, or a number more than two shifts. In item II, the second statement is the inverse of the first statement; they are not logically equivalent.

4. The CORRECT answer is B.
   In item I, any statement in the form "P implies Q" is equivalent to "Not P or Q." In this case, P = A member of the swim team attends practice, and Q = He will compete in the next meet. In item II, "P implies Q" is equivalent to "all P belongs to Q." In this case, P = Engineer wears glasses, and Q = He will know how to use AutoCAD.

5. The CORRECT answer is D. Because the number of high school graduates is so much larger than the number of convicted child abusers, none of the additional pieces of evidence make it reasonably certain that there are convicted abusers within this group of parents.

6. The CORRECT answer is B.
   Statement II is equivalent to "If Mr. Cantwell is reelected to the school board, then school buses are not approved. Statement I assures us that Mr. Cantwell will vote for new school buses. The only logical conclusion is that in spite of Mr. Cantwell's reelection to the board and subsequent vote, approval of the buses was still defeated.

7. The CORRECT answer is B. From Statement II, we conclude that Francis is either a sergeant or a major. If we also know that Stern is a major, we can deduce that Francis is a sergeant. This means that the third person, Jackson, must be a lieutenant.

8. The CORRECT answer is C.
Given that a survival kit contains a gas mask, Statement I assures us that it also contains the anthrax vaccine. If the survival kit near the typist pool only contains two items, than we can conclude that the gas mask in this location cannot contain a third item, namely the anthrax vaccine.

9. The CORRECT answer is C.
The original statement can be written in "P implies Q" form, where P = the heating coil temperature drops below 400 during the twin cycle, and Q = the mechanism shuts itself off. The contrapositive (which must be true) would be "If the mechanism did not shut itself off then the heating coil temperature did not drop below 400." We would then conclude that the temperature was too high and, therefore, the machine did not operate properly.

READING COMPREHENSION
UNDERSTANDING AND INTERPRETING WRITTEN MATERIAL
COMMENTARY

The ability to read, understand, and interpret written materials texts, publications, newspapers, orders, directions, expositions, legal passages is a skill basic to a functioning democracy and to an efficient business or viable government.

That is why almost all examinations—for beginning, middle, and senior levels—test reading comprehension, directly or indirectly.

The reading test measures how well you understand what you read. This is how it is done: You read a paragraph and several statements based on a question. From the statements, you choose the one statement, or answer, that is BEST supported by, or BEST matches, what is said in the paragraph.

SAMPLE QUESTIONS

DIRECTIONS: Each question has five suggested answers, lettered A, B, C, D, and E. Decide which one is the BEST answer. *PRINT THE LETTER OF THE CORRECT ANSWER IN THE SPACE AT THE RIGHT.*

1. The prevention of accidents makes it necessary not only that safety devices be used to guard exposed machinery but also that mechanics be instructed in safety rules which they must follow for their own protection and that the light in the plant be adequate.
The paragraph BEST supports the statement that industrial accidents
    A. are always avoidable
    B. may be due to ignorance
    C. usually result from inadequate machinery
    D. cannot be entirely overcome
    E. result in damage to machinery

1.____

ANALYSIS

Remember what you have to do:
    First: Read the paragraph.
    Second: Decide what the paragraph means.
    Third: Read the five suggested answers.
    Fourth: Select the one answer which BEST matches what the paragraph says or is BEST supported by something in the paragraph. (Sometimes you may have to read the paragraph again in order to be sure which suggested answer is best.)

This paragraph is talking about three steps that should be taken to prevent industrial accidents:
1. Use safety devices on machines
2. Instruct mechanics in safety rules
3. Provide adequate lighting

SELECTION

With this in mind, let's look at each suggested answer. Each one starts with "industrial accidents…"

SUGGESTED ANSWER A
Industrial accidents (A) are always avoidable
(The paragraph talks about how to avoid accidents but does not say that accidents are always avoidable.)

SUGGESTED ANSWER B
Industrial accidents (B) may be due to ignorance.
(One of the steps given in the paragraph to prevent accidents is to instruct mechanics on safety rules. This suggests that lack of knowledge or ignorance of safety rules causes accidents. This suggested answer sounds like a good possibility for being the right answer.)

SUGGESTED ANSWER C
Industrial accidents (C) usually result from inadequate machinery.
(The paragraph does suggest that exposed machines cause accidents, but it doesn't say that it is the usual cause of accidents. The word *usually* makes this a wrong answer.)

SUGGESTED ANSWER D
Industrial accidents (D) cannot be entirely overcome.
(You may know from your own experience that this is a true statement. But that is not what the paragraph is talking about. Therefore, it is NOT the correct answer.)

SUGGESTED ANSWER E
Industrial accidents (E) result in damage to machinery.
(This is a statement that may or may not be true, but, in any case, it is NOT covered by the paragraph.)

Looking back, you see that the one suggested answer of the five given that BEST matches what the paragraph says is:
Industrial accidents (B) may be due to ignorance.
The CORRECT answer then is B.
Be sure you read ALL the possible answers before you make your choice. You may think that none of the five answers is really good, but choose the BEST one of the five.

---

2. Probably few people realize, as they drive on a concrete road, that steel is used to keep the surface flat in spite of the weight of the busses and trucks. Steel bars, deeply embedded in the concrete, provide sinews to take the stresses so that the stresses cannot crack the slab or make it wavy.

2.____

The paragraph BEST supports the statement that a concrete road
- A. is expensive to build
- B. usually cracks under heavy weights
- C. looks like any other road
- D. is used only for heavy traffic
- E. is reinforced with other material

ANALYSIS

This paragraph is commenting on the fact that
1. few people realize, as they drive on a concrete road, that steel is deeply embedded
2. steel keeps the surface flat
3. steel bars enable the road to take the stresses without cracking or becoming wavy

SELECTION

Now read and think about the possible answers:

A. A concrete road is expensive to build.
(Maybe so, but that is not what the paragraph is about.)

B. A concrete road usually cracks under heavy weights.
(The paragraph talks about using steel bars to prevent heavy weights from cracking concrete roads. It says nothing about how usual it is for the roads to crack. The word *usually* makes this suggested answer wrong.)

C. A concrete road looks like any other road.
(This may or may not be true. The important thing to note is that it has nothing to do with what the paragraph is about.)

D. A concrete road is used only for heavy traffic.
(This answer at least has something to do with the paragraph—concrete roads are used with heavy traffic but it does not say "used only.")

E. A concrete road is reinforced with other material.
This choice seems to be the correct one on two counts. First, the paragraph does suggest that concrete roads are made stronger by embedding steel bars in them. This is another way of saying "concrete roads are reinforced with steel bars." Second, by the process of elimination, the other four choices are ruled out as correct answers simply because they do not apply.

You can be sure that not all the reading question will be so easy as these.

SUGGESTIONS FOR ANSWERING READING QUESTIONS

1. Read the paragraph carefully. Then read each suggested answer carefully. Read every word, because often one word can make the difference between a right or wrong answer.

2. Choose that answer which is supported in the paragraph itself. Do not choose an answer which is a correct statement unless it is based on information in the paragraph.

3. Even though a suggested answer has many of the words used in the paragraph, it may still be wrong.

4. Look out for words—such as *always*, *never*, *entirely*, or *only*—which tend to make a suggested answer wrong.

5. Answer first those questions which you can answer most easily. Then, work on the other questions.

6. If you can't figure out the answer to the question, guess.

READING COMPREHENSION
UNDERSTANDING AND INTERPRETING WRITTEN MATERIAL
EXAMINATION SECTION
TEST 1

DIRECTIONS: The following questions are intended to test your ability to read with comprehension and to understand and interpret written materials, particularly legal passages. It will be necessary for you to read each paragraph carefully because the questions are based only on the material contained therein.
Each question has several suggested answers. *PRINT THE LETTER OF THE CORRECT ANSWER IN THE SPACE AT THE RIGHT.*

Questions 1-3.

DIRECTIONS: Answer Questions 1 to 3 *SOLELY* on the basis of the following statement:
Foot patrol has some advantages over all other methods of patrol. Maximum opportunity is provided for observation within range of the senses and for close contact with people and things that enable the patrolman to provide a maximum service as an information source and counselor to the public and as the eyes and ears of the police department. A foot patrolman loses no time in alighting from a vehicle, and the performance of police tasks is not hampered by responsibility for his vehicle while afoot. Foot patrol, however, does not have many of the advantages of a patrol car. Lack of both mobility and immediate communication with headquarters lessens the officer's value in an emergency. The area that he can cover effectively is limited and, therefore, this method of patrol is costly.

1. According to this paragraph, the foot patrolman is the eyes and ears of the police department because he is

    A. in direct contact with the station house
    B. not responsible for a patrol vehicle
    C. able to observe closely conditions on his patrol post
    D. a readily available information source to the public

2. The *MOST* accurate of the following statements concerning the various methods of patrol, according to this paragraph, is that

    A. foot patrol should sometimes be combined with motor patrol
    B. foot patrol is better than motor patrol
    C. helicopter patrol has the same advantages as motor patrol
    D. motor patrol is more readily able to communicate with superior officers in an emergency

3. According to this paragraph, it is *CORRECT* to state that foot patrol is

    A. *economical* since increased mobility makes more rapid action possible
    B. *expensive* since the area that can be patrolled is relatively small
    C. *economical* since vehicle costs need not be considered
    D. *expensive* since giving information to the public is time-consuming

Questions 4-6.

DIRECTIONS: Answer Questions 4 to 6 SOLELY on the basis of the following statement:

All applicants for an original license to operate a catering establishment shall be fingerprinted. This shall include the officers, employees, and stockholders of the company and the members of a partnership. In case of a change, by addition or substitution, occurring during the existence of a license, the person added or substituted shall be fingerprinted. However, in the case of a hotel containing more than 200 rooms, only the officer or manager filing the application is required to be fingerprinted. The police commissioner may also at his discretion exempt the employees and stockholders of any company. The fingerprints shall be taken on one copy of form C.E. 20 and on two copies of C.E. 21. One copy of form C.E. 21 shall accompany the application. Fingerprints are not required with a renewal application.

4. According to this paragraph, an employee added to the payroll of a licensed catering establishment which is not in a hotel, must

   A. always be fingerprinted
   B. be fingerprinted unless he has been previously fingerprinted for another license
   C. be fingerprinted unless exempted by the police commissioner
   D. be fingerprinted only if he is the manager or an officer of the company

5. According to this paragraph, it would be MOST accurate to state that

   A. form C.E. 20 must accompany a renewal application
   B. form C.E. 21 must accompany all applications
   C. form C.E. 21 must accompany an original application
   D. both forms C.E. 20 and C.E. 21 must accompany all applications

6. A hotel of 270 rooms has applied for a license to operate a catering establishment on the premises. According to the instructions for fingerprinting given in this paragraph, the

   A. officers, employees, and stockholders shall be fingerprinted
   B. officers and manager shall be fingerprinted
   C. employees shall be fingerprinted
   D. officer filing the application shall be fingerprinted

Questions 7-9.

DIRECTIONS: Answer Questions 7 to 9 SOLELY on the basis of the following statement:

It is difficult to instill in young people inner controls on aggressive behavior in a world marked by aggression. The slum child's environment, full of hostility, stimulates him to delinquency; he does that which he sees about him. The time to act against delinquency is before it is committed. It is clear that juvenile delinquency, especially when it is committed in groups or gangs, leads almost inevitably to an adult criminal life unless it is checked at once. The first signs of vandalism and disregard for the comfort, health, and property of the community should be considered as storm warnings which cannot be ignored. The delinquent's first crime has the underlying element of testing the law and its ability to hit back.

7. A *suitable* title for this entire paragraph based on the material it contains is: 7._____

   A. The Need for Early Prevention of Juvenile Delinquency
   B. Juvenile Delinquency as a Cause of Slums
   C. How Aggressive Behavior Prevents Juvenile Delinquency
   D. The Role of Gangs in Crime

8. According to this paragraph, an *INITIAL* act of juvenile crime *usually* involves a(n) 8._____

   A. group or gang activity
   B. theft of valuable property
   C. test of the strength of legal authority
   D. act of physical violence

9. According to this paragraph, acts of juvenile delinquency are *most likely* to lead to a criminal career when they are 9._____

   A. acts of vandalism
   B. carried out by groups or gangs
   C. committed in a slum environment
   D. such as to impair the health of the neighborhood

Questions 10-12.

DIRECTIONS: Answer Questions 10 to 12 *SOLELY* on the basis of the following statement:
The police laboratory performs a valuable service in crime investigation by assisting in the reconstruction of criminal action and by aiding in the identification of persons and things. When studied by a technician, physical things found at crime scenes often reveal facts useful in identifying the criminal and in determining what has occurred. The nature of substances to be examined and the character of the examinations to be made vary so widely that the services of a large variety of skilled scientific persons are needed in crime investigations. To employ such a complete staff and to provide them with equipment and standards needed for all possible analyses and comparisons is beyond the means and the needs of any but the largest police departments. The search of crime scenes for physical evidence also calls for the services of specialists supplied with essential equipment and assigned to each tour of duty so as to provide service at any hour.

10. If a police department employs a large staff of technicians of various types in its laboratory, it will affect crime investigation to the extent that 10._____

    A. most crimes will be speedily solved
    B. identification of criminals will be aided
    C. search of crime scenes for physical evidence will become of less importance
    D. investigation by police officers will not usually be required

11. According to this paragraph, the *MOST* complete study of objects found at the scenes of crimes is 11._____

    A. always done in all large police departments
    B. based on assigning one technician to each tour of duty
    C. probably done only in large police departments
    D. probably done in police departments of communities with low crime rates

12. According to this paragraph, a large variety of skilled technicians is useful in criminal investigations because

    A. crimes cannot be solved without their assistance as a part of the police team
    B. large police departments need large staffs
    C. many different kinds of tests on various substances can be made
    D. the police cannot predict what methods may be tried by wily criminals

Questions 13-14.

DIRECTIONS: Answer Questions 13 and 14 SOLELY on the basis of the following statement:
The emotionally unstable person is always potentially a dangerous criminal, who causes untold misery to other persons and is a source of considerable trouble and annoyance to law enforcement officials. Like his fellow criminals he will be a menace to society as long as he is permitted to be at large. Police activities against him serve to sharpen his wits, and imprisonment gives him the opportunity to learn from others how to commit more serious crimes when he is released. This criminal's mental structure makes it impossible for him to profit by his experience with the police officials, by punishment of any kind or by sympathetic understanding and treatment by well-intentioned persons, professional and otherwise.

13. According to the above paragraph, the MOST accurate of the following statements concerning the relationship between emotional instability and crime is that

    A. emotional instability is proof of criminal activities
    B. the emotionally unstable person can become a criminal
    C. all dangerous criminals are emotionally unstable
    D. sympathetic understanding will prevent the emotionally unstable person from becoming a criminal

14. According to the above paragraph, the effect of police activities on the emotionally unstable criminal is that

    A. police activities aid this type of criminal to reform
    B. imprisonment tends to deter this type of criminal from committing future crimes
    C. contact with the police serves to assist sympathetic understanding and medical treatment
    D. police methods against this type of criminal develop him for further unlawful acts

Questions 15-17.

DIRECTIONS: Answer Questions 15 to 17 SOLELY on the basis of the following statement:
Proposals to license gambling operations are based on the belief that the human desire to gamble cannot be suppressed and, therefore, it should be licensed and legalized with the people sharing in the profits, instead of allowing the underworld to benefit. If these proposals are sincere, then it is clear that only one is worthwhile at all. Legalized gambling should be completely controlled and operated by the state with all the profits used for its citizens. A state agency should be set up to operate and control the gambling business. It should be as completely removed from politics as possible. In view of the inherent nature of the gambling business, with its close relationship to lawlessness and crime, only a man of the highest integrity should be eligible to become head of this agency. However, state gambling would encourage mass gambling with its attending social and economic evils in the same manner as other forms of legal gambling; but there is no justification whatever for the business of gambling to be legalized and then permitted to operate for private profit or for the benefit of any political organization.

15. The CENTRAL thought of this paragraph may be correctly expressed as the

    A. need to legalize gambling in the state
    B. state operation of gambling for the benefit of the people
    C. need to license private gambling establishments
    D. evils of gambling

16. According to this paragraph, a problem of legalized gambling which will *still* occur if the state operates the gambling business is

    A. the diversion of profits from gambling to private use
    B. that the amount of gambling will tend to diminish
    C. the evil effects of any form of mass gambling
    D. the use of gambling revenues for illegal purposes

17. According to this paragraph, to legalize the business of gambling would be

    A. *justified* because gambling would be operated only by a man of the highest integrity
    B. *justified* because this would eliminate politics
    C. *unjustified* under any conditions because the human desire to gamble cannot be suppressed
    D. *unjustified* if operated for private or political profit

Questions 18-20.

DIRECTIONS: Answer Questions 18 to 20 SOLELY on the basis of the following statement:
Whenever, in the course of the performance of their duties in an emergency, members of the force operate the emergency power switch at any location on the transit system and thereby remove power from portions of the track, or they are on the scene where this has been done, they will bear in mind that, although power is removed, further dangers exist; namely, that a train may coast into the area even though the power is off, or that the rails may be energized by a train which may be in a position to transfer electricity from a live portion of the third rail through its shoe beams. Employees must look in each direction before stepping upon, crossing, or standing close to tracks, being particularly careful not to come into contact with the third rail.

18. According to this paragraph, whenever an emergency occurs which has resulted in operating the emergency power switch, it is MOST accurate to state that

    A. power is shut off and employees may perform their duties in complete safety
    B. there may still be power in a portion of the third rail
    C. the switch will not operate if a portion of the track has been broken
    D. trains are not permitted to stop in the area of the emergency

19. An *important* precaution which this paragraph urges employees to follow after operating the emergency power switch, is to

    A. look carefully in both directions before stepping near the rails
    B. inspect the nearest train which has stopped to see if the power is on
    C. examine the third rail to see if the power is on
    D. check the emergency power switch to make sure it has operated properly

20. A trackman reports to you, a patrolman, that a dead body is lying on the road bed. You operate the emergency power switch. A train which has been approaching comes to a stop near the scene.
In order to act in accordance with the instructions in the above paragraph, you *should*

   A. climb down to the road bed and remove the body
   B. direct the train motorman to back up to the point where his train will not be in position to transfer electricity through its shoe beams
   C. carefully cross over the road bed to the body, avoiding the third rail and watching for train movements
   D. have the train motorman check to see if power is on before crossing to the tracks

21. The treatment to be given the offender cannot alter the fact of his offense; but we can take measures to reduce the chances of similar acts in the future. We should banish the criminal, not in order to exact revenge nor directly to encourage reform, but to deter him and others from further illegal attacks on society.
According to this paragraph, the *PRINCIPAL* reason for punishing criminals is to

   A. prevent the commission of future crimes
   B. remove them from society
   C. avenge society
   D. teach them that crime does not pay

22. Even the most comprehensive and best substantiated summaries of the total volume of criminal acts would not contribute greatly to an understanding of the varied social and biological factors which are sometimes assumed to enter into crime causation, nor would they indicate with any degree of precision the needs of police forces in combating crime.
According to this statement,

   A. crime statistics alone do not determine the needs of police forces in combating crime
   B. crime statistics are essential to a proper understanding of the social factors of crime
   C. social and biological factors which enter into crime causation have little bearing on police needs
   D. a knowledge of the social and biological factors of crime is essential to a proper understanding of crime statistics

23. The policeman's art consists of applying and enforcing a multitude of laws and ordinances in such degree or proportion and in such manner that the greatest degree of social protection will be secured. The degree of enforcement and the method of application will vary with each neighborhood and community.
According to the foregoing paragraph,

   A. each neighborhood or community must judge for itself to what extent the law is to be enforced
   B. a policeman should only enforce those laws which are designed to give the greatest degree of social protection
   C. the manner and intensity of law enforcement is not necessarily the same in all communities
   D. all laws and ordinances must be enforced in a community with the same degree of intensity

24. Police control in the sense of regulating the details of police operations, involves such matters as the technical means for so organizing the available personnel that competent police leadership, when secured, can operate effectively. It is concerned not so much with the extent to which popular controls can be trusted to guide and direct the course of police protection as with the administrative relationships which should exist between the component parts of the polie organism. According to the foregoing statement, police control is

    A. solely a matter of proper personnel assignment
    B. the means employed to guide and direct the course of police protection
    C. principally concerned with the administrative relationships between units of a police organization
    D. the sum total of means employed in rendering police protection

25. Police Department Rule 5 states that a Deputy Commissioner acting as Police Commissioner shall carry out the orders of the Police Commissioner, previously given, and such orders shall not, except in cases of extreme emergency, be countermanded. This means, most nearly, that, except in cases of extreme emergency,

    A. the orders given by a Deputy Commissioner acting as Police Commissioner may not be revoked
    B. a Deputy Commissioner acting as Police Commissioner should not revoke orders previously given by the Police Commissioner
    C. a Deputy Commissioner acting as Police Commissioner is vested with the same authority to issue orders as the Police Commissioner himself
    D. only a Deputy Commissioner acting as Police Commissioner may issue orders in the absence of the Police Commissioner himself

---

KEY (CORRECT ANSWERS)

1.	C	11.	C
2.	D	12.	C
3.	B	13.	B
4.	C	14.	D
5.	C	15.	B
6.	D	16.	C
7.	A	17.	D
8.	C	18.	B
9.	B	19.	A
10.	B	20.	C

21.	A
22.	A
23.	C
24.	C
25.	B

TEST 2

Questions 1-2.

DIRECTIONS: Answer Questions 1 and 2 SOLELY on the basis of the following statement:

The medical examiner may contribute valuable data to the investigator of fires which cause fatalities. By careful examination of the bodies of any victims, he not only establishes cause of death, but may also furnish, in many instances, answers to questions relating to the identity of the victim and the source and origin of the fire. The medical examiner is of greatest value to law enforcement agencies because he is able to determine the exact cause of death through an examination of tissue of apparent arson victims. Thorough study of a burned body or even of parts of a burned body will frequently yield information which illuminates the problems confronting the arson investigator and the police.

1. According to the above paragraph, the MOST important task of the medical examiner in the investigation of arson is to obtain information concerning the

   A. identity of arsonists
   B. cause of death
   C. identity of victims
   D. source and origin of fires

2. The CENTRAL thought of the above paragraph is that the medical examiner aids in the solution of crimes of arson when

   A. a person is burnt to death
   B. identity of the arsonist is unknown
   C. the cause of the fire is known
   D. trained investigators are not available

Questions 3-6.

DIRECTIONS: Answer Questions 3 to 6 SOLELY on the basis of the following statement:

A foundling is an abandoned child whose identity is unknown. Desk officers shall direct the delivery, by a policewoman, if available, of foundlings actually or apparently under two years of age, to the Foundling Hospital, or if actually or apparently two years of age or over, to the Children's Center. In all other cases of dependent or neglected children, other than foundlings, requiring shelter, desk officers shall provide for obtaining such shelter as follows: between 9 a.m. and 5 p.m., Monday through Friday, by telephone direct to the Bureau of Child Welfare, in order to ascertain the shelter to which the child shall be sent; at all other times, direct the delivery of a child actually or apparently under two years of age to the Foundling Hospital, or, if the child is actually or apparently two years of age or over, to the Children's Center.

3. According to this paragraph, it would be MOST correct to state that

   A. a foundling as well as a neglected child may be delivered to the Foundling Hospital
   B. a foundling but not a neglected child may be delivered to the Children's Center
   C. a neglected child requiring shelter, regardless of age, may be delivered to the Bureau of Child Welfare
   D. the Bureau of Child Welfare may determine the shelter to which a foundling may be delivered

4. According to this paragraph, the desk officer shall provide for obtaining shelter for a neglected child, apparently under two years of age, by

   A. directing its delivery to the Children's Center if occurrence is on a Monday between 9 a.m. and 5 p.m.
   B. telephoning the Bureau of Child Welfare if occurrence is on a Sunday
   C. directing its delivery to the Foundling Hospital if occurrence is on a Wednesday at 4 p.m.
   D. telephoning the Bureau of Child Welfare if occurrence is at 10 a.m. on a Friday

5. According to this paragraph, the desk officer should direct delivery to the Foundling Hospital of any child who is

   A. actually under 2 years of age and requires shelter
   B. apparently under two years of age and is neglected or dependent
   C. actually 2 years of age and is a foundling
   D. apparently under 2 years of age and has been abandoned

6. A 12-year-old neglected child requiring shelter is brought to a police station on Thursday at 2 p.m. Such a child should be sent to

   A. a shelter selected by the Bureau of Child Welfare
   B. a shelter selected by the desk officer
   C. the Children's Center
   D. the Foundling Hospital when a brother or sister, under 2 years of age, also requires shelter

Questions 7-9.

DIRECTIONS: Answer Questions 7 to 9 *SOLELY* on the basis of the following statement:
In addition to making the preliminary investigation of crimes, patrolmen should serve as eyes, ears, and legs for the detective division. The patrol division may be used for surveillance, to serve warrants and bring in suspects and witnesses, and to perform a number of routine tasks for the detectives which will increase the time available for tasks that require their special skills and facilities. It is to the advantage of individual detectives, as well as of the detective division, to have patrolmen working in this manner; more cases are cleared by arrest and a greater proportion of stolen property is recovered when, in addition to the detective regularly assigned, a number of patrolmen also work on the case. Detectives may stimulate the interest and participation of patrolmen by keeping them currently informed of the presence, identity, or description, hangouts, associates, vehicles and method of operation of each criminal known to be in the community.

7. According to this paragraph, a patrolman should

   A. assist the detective in certain of his routine functions
   B. be considered for assignment as a detective on the basis of his patrol performance
   C. leave the scene once a detective arrives
   D. perform as much of the detective's duties as time permits

8. According to this paragraph, patrolmen should aid detectives by

   A. accepting assignments from detectives which give promise of recovering stolen property
   B. making arrests of witnesses for the detective's interrogation
   C. performing all special investigative work for detectives
   D. producing for questioning individuals who may aid the detective in his investigation

9. According to this paragraph, detectives can keep patrolmen interested by

   A. ascertaining that patrolmen are doing investigative work properly
   B. having patrolmen directly under his supervision during an investigation
   C. informing patrolmen of the value of their efforts in crime prevention
   D. supplying the patrolmen with information regarding known criminals in the community

Questions 10-11.

DIRECTIONS: Answer Questions 10 and 11 *SOLELY* on the basis of the following statement:
State motor vehicle registration departments should and do play a vital role in the prevention and detection of automobile thefts. The combatting of theft is, in fact, one of the primary purposes of the registration of motor vehicles. As of recent date, there were approximately 61,309,000 motor vehicles registered in the United States. That same year some 200,000 of them were stolen. All but 6 percent have been or will be recovered. This is a very high recovery ratio compared to the percentage of recovery of other stolen personal property. The reason for this is that automobiles are carefully identified by the manufacturers and carefully registered by many of the states.

10. The *CENTRAL* thought of this paragraph is that there is a close relationship between the

    A. number of automobiles registered in the United States *and* the number stolen
    B. prevention of automobile thefts *and* the effectiveness of police departments in the United States
    C. recovery of stolen automobiles *and* automobile registration
    D. recovery of stolen automobiles *and* of other stolen property

11. According to this paragraph, the high recovery ratio for stolen automobiles is due to

    A. state registration and manufacturer identification of motor vehicles
    B. successful prevention of automobile thefts by state motor vehicle departments
    C. the fact that only 6% of stolen vehicles are not properly registered
    D. the high number of motor vehicles registered in the United States

Questions 12-15.

DIRECTIONS: Answer Questions 12 to 15 *SOLELY* on the basis of the following statement:
It is not always understood that the term "physical evidence" embraces any and all objects, living or inanimate. A knife, gun, signature, or burglar tool is immediately recognized as physical evidence. Less often is it considered that dust, microscopic fragments of all types, even an odor, may equally be physical evidence and often the most important of all. It is well established that the most useful types of physical evidence are generally microscopic in dimensions, that is, not noticeable by the eye and, therefore, most likely to be overlooked by

the criminal and by the investigator. For this reason, microscopic evidence persists for months or years after all other evidence has been removed and found inconclusive. Naturally, there are limitations to the time of collecting microscopic evidence as it may be lost or decayed. The exercise of judgment as to the possibility or profit of delayed action in collecting the evidence is a field in which the expert investigator should judge.

12. The *one* of the following which the above paragraph does *NOT* consider to be physical evidence is a

    A. criminal thought
    B. minute speck of dust
    C. raw onion smell
    D. typewritten note

13. According to the above paragraph, the re-checking of the scene of a crime

    A. is *useless* when performed years after the occurrence of the crime
    B. is *advisable* chiefly in crimes involving physical violence
    C. *may turn up* microscopic evidence of value
    D. *should be delayed* if the microscopic evidence is not subject to decay or loss

14. According to the above paragraph, the criminal investigator *should*

    A. give most of his attention to weapons used in the commission of the crime
    B. ignore microscopic evidence until a request is received from the laboratory
    C. immediately search for microscopic evidence and ignore the more visible objects
    D. realize that microscopic evidence can be easily overlooked

15. According to the above paragraph,

    A. a delay in collecting evidence must definitely diminish its value to the investigator
    B. microscopic evidence exists for longer periods of time than other physical evidence
    C. microscopic evidence is generally the most useful type of physical evidence
    D. physical evidence is likely to be overlooked by the criminal and by the investigator

Questions 16-18.

DIRECTIONS: Answer Questions 16 to 18 *SOLELY* on the basis of the following statement:
Sometimes, but not always, firing a gun leaves a residue of nitrate particles on the hands. This fact is utilized in the paraffin test which consists of applying melted paraffin and gauze to the fingers, hands, and wrists of a suspect until a cast of approximately 1/8 of an inch is built up. The heat of the paraffin causes the pores of the skin to open and release any particles embedded in them. The paraffin cast is then removed and tested chemically for nitrate particles. In addition to gunpowder, fertilizers, tobacco ashes, matches, and soot are also common sources of nitrates on the hands.

16. Assume that the paraffin test has been given to a person suspected of firing a gun and that nitrate particles have been found. It would be *CORRECT* to conclude that the suspect

    A. is guilty
    B. is innocent
    C. may be guilty or innocent
    D. is probably guilty

17. In testing for the presence of gunpowder particles on human hands, the characteristic of paraffin which makes it MOST serviceable is that it 17.___

    A. causes the nitrate residue left by a fired gun to adhere to the gauze
    B. is waterproof
    C. melts at a low temperature
    D. helps to distinguish between gunpowder nitrates and other types

18. According to the above paragraph, in the paraffin test, the nitrate particles are removed from the pores because the paraffin 18.___

    A. enlarges the pores   B. contracts the pores
    C. reacts chemically with nitrates D. dissolves the particles

Questions 19-21.

DIRECTIONS: Answer Questions 19 to 21 SOLELY on the basis of the following statement:
     Pickpockets operate most effectively when there are prospective victims in either heavily congested areas or in lonely places. In heavily populated areas, the large number of people about them covers the activities of these thieves. In lonely spots, they have the advantage of working unobserved. The main factor in the pickpocket's success is the selection of the "right" victim, A pickpocket's victim must, at the time of the crime, be inattentive, distracted, or unconscious. If any of these conditions exist, and if the pickpocket is skilled in his operations, the stage is set for a successful larceny. With the coming of winter, the crowds move south-ward—and so do most of the pickpockets. However, some pickpockets will remain in certain areas all year around. They will concentrate on theater districts, bus and railroad terminals, hotels or large shopping centers. A complete knowledge of the methods of this type of criminal and the ability to recognize them come only from long years of experience in performing patient surveillance and trailing of them. This knowledge is essential for the effective control and apprehension of this type of thief.

19. According to this paragraph, the pickpocket is LEAST likely to operate in a 19.___

    A. baseball park with a full capacity attendance
    B. station in an outlying area late at night
    C. moderately crowded dance hall
    D. over-crowded department store

20. According to this paragraph, the one of the following factors which is NOT necessary for the successful operation of the pickpocket is that 20.___

    A. he be proficient in the operations required to pick pockets
    B. the "right" potential victims be those who have been the subject of such a theft previously
    C. his operations be hidden from the view of others
    D. the potential victim be unaware of the actions of the pickpocket

21. According to this paragraph, it would be MOST correct to conclude that police officers who are successful in apprehending pickpockets 21.___

    A. are generralling those who have had lengthy experience in recognizing all types of criminals
    B. must, by intuition, be able to recognize potential "right" victims

C. must follow the pickpockets in their southward movement
D. must have acquired specific knowledge and skills in this field

Questions 22-23.

DIRECTIONS: Answer Questions 22 and 23 *SOLELY* on the basis of the following statement:
For many years, slums had been recognized as breeding disease, juvenile delinquency, and crime which not only threatened the health and welfare of the people who lived there, but also weakened the structure of society as a whole. As far back as 1834, a sanitary inspection report in the city pointed out the connection between insanitary, overcrowded housing and the spread of epidemics. Down through the years, evidence of slum-produced evils accumulated as the slums themselves continued to spread. This spread of slums was nationwide. Its symptoms and its ill effects were peculiar to no locality, but were characteristic of the country as a whole and imperiled the national welfare.

22. According to this paragraph, people who live in slum dwellings

    A. cause slums to become worse
    B. are threatened by disease and crime
    C. create bad housing
    D. are the chief source of crime in the country

23. According to this paragraph, the effects of juvenile delinquency and crime in slum areas were

    A. to destroy the structure of society
    B. noticeable in all parts of the country
    C. a chief cause of the spread of slums
    D. to spread insanitary conditions in the city

Questions 24-25.

DIRECTIONS: Questions 24 and 25 pertain to the following section of the Penal Law:
Section 1942. A person who, after having been three times convicted within this state, of felonies or attempts to commit felonies, or under the law of any other state, government or country, of crimes which if committed within this state would be felonious, commits a felony, other than murder, first or second degree, or treason, within this state, shall be sentenced upon conviction of such fourth, or subsequent, offense to imprisonment in a state prison for an indeterminate term the minimum of which shall be not less than the maximum term provided for first offenders for the crime for which the individual has been convicted, but, in any event, the minimum term upon conviction for a felony as the fourth, or subsequent, offense, shall be not less than fifteen years, and the maximum thereof shall be his natural life.

24. Under the terms of the above stated portion of Section 1942 of the Penal Law, a person must receive the increased punishment therein provided *if*

    A. he is convicted of a felony and has been three times previously convicted of felonies
    B. he has been three times previously convicted of felonies, regardless of the nature of his present conviction

C. his fourth conviction is for murder, first or second degree, or treason
D. he has previously been convicted three times of murder, first or second degree, or treason

25. Under the terms of the above stated portion of Section 1942 of the Penal Law, a person convicted of a felony for which the penalty is imprisonment for a term not to exceed ten years, and who has been three times previously convicted of felonies in this state, shall be sentenced to a term the *minimum* of which shall be

 A. ten years   B. fifteen years
 C. indeterminate   D. his natural life

KEY (CORRECT ANSWERS)

1.	B	11.	A
2.	A	12.	A
3.	A	13.	C
4.	D	14.	D
5.	D	15.	C
6.	A	16.	C
7.	A	17.	A
8.	D	18.	A
9.	D	19.	C
10.	C	20.	B

21. D
22. B
23. B
24. A
25. B

OFFICE RECORD KEEPING
EXAMINATION SECTION
TEST 1

DIRECTIONS: Each question or incomplete statement is followed by several suggested answers or completions. Select the one that BEST answers the question or completes the statement. *PRINT THE LETTER OF THE CORRECT ANSWER IN THE SPACE AT THE RIGHT.*

Questions 1-5.

DIRECTIONS: Questions 1 through 5 are to be answered on the basis of the following chart to check for address and zip code errors.

    A. No errors
    B. Address only
    C. Zip code only
    D. Both

	Correct List Address	Zip Code	List to be Checked Address	Zip Code	
1.	44-A Western Avenue Bethesda, MD	65564	44-A Western Avenue Bethesda, MD	65654	1.____
2.	567 Opera Lane Jackson, MO	28218	567 Opera Lane Jacksen, MO	28218	2.____
3.	200 W. Jannine Dr. Missoula, MT	30707	200 W. Jannine Dr. Missoula, MT	30307	3.____
4.	28 Champaline Dr. Reno, NV	34101	28 Champaine Way Reno, NV	43101	4.____
5.	65156 Rodojo Parsimony, KY	44590-7326	65156 Rodojo Parsimony, KY	44590-7326	5.____

6. When alphabetized correctly, which of the following would be second?   6.____
    A. flame   B. herring   C. decadence   D. emoticon

7. Which one of the following letters is as far after E as K is before R in the alphabet?   7.____
    A. J   B. K   C. H   D. M

8. How many pairs of the following sets of numbers are exactly alike?   8.____

    134232   123456   432512   561343
    564643   432123   132439   438318

    A. 0   B. 2   C. 3   D. 4

9. When alphabetized correctly, which of the following would be FOURTH? 9.____
 A. microcosm   B. natural   C. lithe   D. nature

10. When alphabetized correctly, which of the following would be THIRD? 10.____
 A. exoskeleton   B. euthanize   C. Europe   D. eurythmic

11. Which one of the following letters is as far before T as S is after I in the alphabet? 11.____
 A. j   B. K   C. M   D. N

12. How many pairs of the following sets of letters are exactly ALIKE? 12.____
    GIHEKE   GIHEKE
    KIWNEB   KWINEB
    PQMZJI   PMQZJI
    OPZIBS   OBZIBS
    PONEHE   POENHE

 A. 0   B. 1   C. 2   D. 4

13. When alphabetized correctly, which of the following would be FIRST? 13.____
 A. Catalina   B. catcher   C. caustic   D. curious

14. Which of the following letters is as far after D as U is after B in the alphabet? 14.____
 A. R   B. V   C. W   D. Z

Questions 15-19.

DIRECTIONS: Use the following information and chart to complete Questions 15 through 19.

Every theft reported to an adjuster needs to be assigned a six-letter code containing the following:

   First Letter: Type of theft
   Second Letter: Witnesses
   Third Letter: Value of stolen item
   Fourth Letter: Location
   Fifth Letter: Time of theft
   Sixth Letter: Elapsed between theft and report

   Type of Theft: Witnesses
   A. Breaking and Entering   A. None
   B. Retail Theft   B. 1 witness
   C. Armed robbery   C. Multiple witnesses
   D. Grand Theft Auto   D. Security camera

3 (#1)

Location
A. Single Family Home
B. Apartment Building
C. Store
D. Office
E. Vehicle
F. Public Space (Parking Garage, Park, etc.)

Time Elapsed Between Theft and Report
A. 0-1 hour
B. 1-4 hours
C. 4-12 hours
D. 12-24 hours
E. 24 Hours

Time of Theft
A. 7 AM – 1 PM
B. 1 PM – 6 PM
C. 6 PM – 11 PM
D. 11 PM – 3 AM
E. 3 AM – 7 AM

Value of Stolen Items
A. $0-$100
B. $101-$250
C. $251-$500
D. $500-$1000
E. $1001-$5000
F. $5000 or more

15. At 9:30 PM, $175 worth of clothing was stolen from a store. The crime was reported right away by a single store associate. Which of the following would be the CORRECT code?
    A. BCCABB   B. BBBCCA   C. ACCBAB   D. CBCABB

16. A Crossover vehicle worth $4,500 was stolen from a park at approximately 6:45 AM this morning. It was reported stolen at 11:00 AM later that morning by the owner. There were no witnesses. What is the CORRECT code?
    A. DEECAF   B. CFECAE   C. DEFECA   D. DAEFEC

17. Although it was just reported, a breaking and entering occurred 5 days ago at 1:30 AM, according to security cameras that recorded the theft at the accounting firm. Although locks and doors were damaged, nothing was stolen. Which of the following would be the CORRECT code?
    A. ADDEEA   B. ADDDAE   C. ADADDE   D. ADEADE

18. Jill Wagner was held at knifepoint this morning at 11:30 AM when she was walking out of her apartment complex. The thief demanded money, and she gave him $54. She was the only witness and reported the crime immediately. Which of the following would be the CORRECT code?
    A. CBABAA   B. BBABAA   C. CBBABB   D. ABBBCA

19. An artifact worth $5,500 was stolen from the home of Chad Judea this early evening while he was out to dinner from 5:30 PM to 6 PM. When he arrived home at 6 PM, he immediately called the police. There were no witnesses. Which of the following would be the CORRECT code?
    A. AABBAF   B. AABFAF   C. AABABF   D. AAFABA

20. Diatribe means MOST NEARLY
    A. argument   B. cooperation   C. delicate   D. arrogance

4 (#1)

21. Vitriolic means MOST NEARLY 21.____
    A. flammable   B. fearful   C. spiteful   D. asinine

22. Aplomb means MOST NEARLY 22.____
    A. self-righteous   B. respectable   C. dispirited   D. self-confidence

23. Pervicacious means MOST NEARLY 23.____
    A. rotten   B. immoral   C. stubborn   D. immortal

24. Detrimental means MOST NEARLY 24.____
    A. valuable   B. selfish   C. hopeless   D. harmful

25. Heinous means MOST NEARLY 25.____
    A. sweating   B. glorious   C. atrocious   D. moderate

KEY (CORRECT ANSWERS)

1.	C		11.	A
2.	B		12.	B
3.	C		13.	A
4.	D		14.	C
5.	A		15.	B
6.	D		16.	D
7.	B		17.	C
8.	A		18.	A
9.	D		19.	D
10.	B		20.	A

21. C
22. D
23. C
24. D
25. C

TEST 2

DIRECTIONS: Each question or incomplete statement is followed by several suggested answers or completions. Select the one that BEST answers the question or completes the statement. *PRINT THE LETTER OF THE CORRECT ANSWER IN THE SPACE AT THE RIGHT.*

Questions 1-7.

DIRECTIONS: In answering Questions 1 through 7, you will be presented with analogies (known as word relationships). Select the answer choice that BEST completes the analogy.

1. Coordinated is related to movement as speech is related to 1.____
   A. predictive   B. rapid   C. prophetic   D. articulate

2. Pottery is related to shard as wood is related to 2.____
   A. acorn   B. chair   C. smoke   D. kiln

3. Poverty is related to money as famine is related to 3.____
   A. nourishment   B. infirmity   C. illness   D. care

4. Farmland is related to arable as waterway is related to 4.____
   A. impenetrable   B. maneuverable
   C. fertile   D. deep

5. 19 is related to 17 as 37 is related to 5.____
   A. 39   B. 36   C. 34   D. 31

6. Cup is related to lip as bird is related to 6.____
   A. beak   B. grass   C. forest   D. bush

7. ZRYQ is related to KCJB as PWOV is related to 7.____
   A. GBHA   B. ISJT   C. ELDK   D. EOFP

Questions 8-12.

DIRECTIONS: In answering Questions 8 through 12, each of the questions has a group. Find out which one of the given alternatives will be another member of that group.

8. Springfield, Sacramento, Tallahassee 8.____
   A. Buffalo   B. Bangor   C. Pittsburgh   D. Providence

9. Lock, Shut, Fasten 9.____
   A. Window   B. Iron   C. Door   D. Block

10. Pathology, Radiology, Ophthalmology 10.____
    A. Zoology   B. Hematology   C. Geology   D. Biology

11. Karate, Jujitsu, Boxing 11._____
    A. Polo   B. Pole-vault   C. Judo   D. Swimming

12. Newspaper, Hoarding, Television 12._____
    A. Press   B. Rumor   C. Media   D. Broadcast

Questions 13-18.

DIRECTIONS: Questions 13 through 18 are to be answered on the basis of the following pie chart.

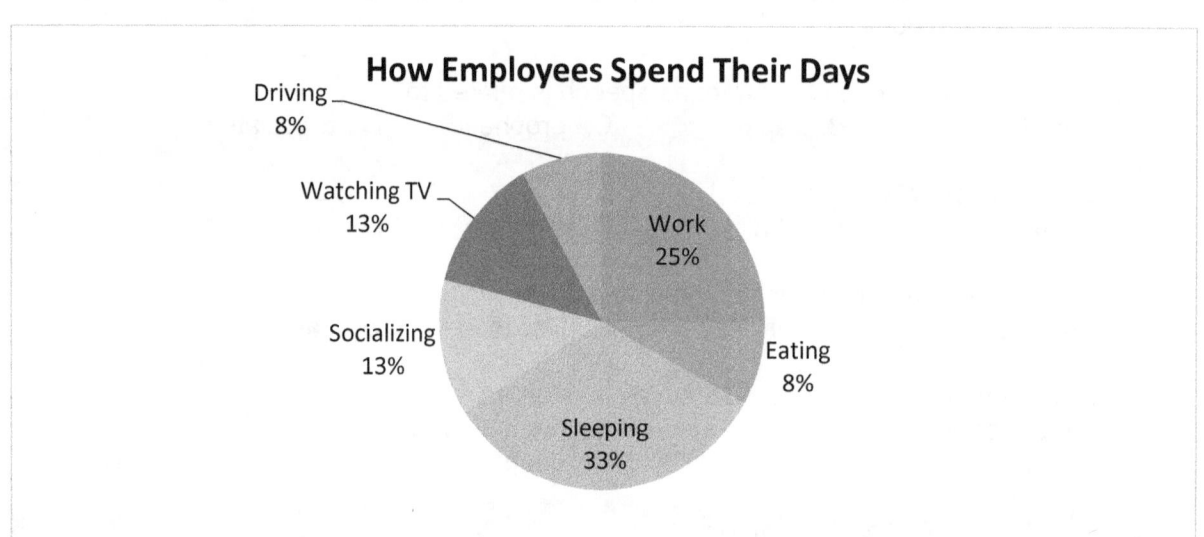

13. Approximately how many hours a day are spent eating? 13._____
    A. 2 hours   B. 5 hours   C. 1 hour   D. 30 minutes

14. According to the graph, for each 48 hour period, about how many hours are spent socializing and watching TV? 14._____
    A. 9 hours   B. 6 hours   C. 12 hours   D. 3 hours

15. If an employee ate two-thirds of their meals at a restaurant, what percentage of the total day is spent eating at home? 15._____
    A. 2.5%   B. 5.3%   C. 8%   D. 1.4%

16. About how many hours a day are spent working and sleeping? 16._____
    A. 7   B. 10   C. 12   D. 14

17. Which of the following equations could be used to figure out how much time an employee spends watching TV during a week? T equals the total amount of time watching TV during the week. 17._____
    A. T = 13% x 24 x 7   B. T = 24 x 13 x 7
    C. T = 24/13% x 7   D. T = 1.3 x 7 x 24

18. How many hours a week does the average employee spend socializing? 18._____
    A. 20   B. 22   C. 23   D. 24

Questions 19-25.

DIRECTIONS: Questions 19 through 25 are to be answered on the basis of the following charts.

DIAL DIRECT	WEEKDAY FULL RATE		EVENING 40% DISCOUNT		WEEKEND 60% DISCOUNT	
SAMPLE RATES FROM SEATTLE TO	FIRST MINUTE	EACH ADDITIONAL MINUTE	FIRST MINUTE	EACH ADDITIONAL MINUTE	FIRST MINUTE	EACH ADDITIONAL MINUTE
Savannah, GA	.52	.23	.31	.14	.21	.08
Providence, RI	.52	.223	.31	.14	.21	.08
Golden, CO	.52	.23	.31	.14	.21	.08
Indianapolis, IN	.48	.19	.29	.11	.19	.07
San Diego, CA	.54	.24	.32	.14	.22	.09
Tallahassee, FL	.54	.24	.32	.14	.22	.09
Milwaukee, WI	.57	.27	.34	.16	.23	.09
Minneapolis, MN	.49	.22	.29	.13	.20	.08
Baton Rouge, LA	.52	.23	.31	.14	.21	.08
Buffalo, NY	.52	.23	.31	.14	.21	.08
Annapolis, MD	.54	.24	.32	.14	.22	.09
Washington, DC	.52	.23	.31	.14	.21	.08

OPERATOR ASSISTED		
STATION-TO-STATION		PERSON-TO-PERSON
1 – 10 MILES	$.75	$3.00 FEE FOR ALL MILEAGES
11 - 22 MILES	$1.10	*NOTE: Add to this base charge – the minute rates from the above chart
23-3000 MILES	$1.55	

19. What is the price of a 6-minute dial direct call to Annapolis, MD when you call on a weekend?
    A. $0.59   B. $0.54   C. $0.67   D. $0.49

20. What is the difference in cost between a 10 minute dial direct to Buffalo, NY and a 10 minute person-to-person call to Buffalo, NY?
    A. $1.55   B. $3.00   C. $0.55   D. $4.55

21. What is the price of a 15-minute operator-assisted Station-to-Station call to Indianapolis, IN on a Monday at noon?
    A. $3.74   B. $7.80   C. $3.45   D. $4.69

22. What is the difference in price between an 11-minute dial direct call to Milwaukee, WI at 11:00 AM on a Wednesday and the same call made at 9 PM that night?
    A. $2.27   B. $3.00   C. $1.55   D. $1.336

19.____
20.____
21.____
22.____

4 (#2)

23. Which of the following is NOT a type of charge for a dial direct call? 23._____
    A. Holiday   B. Evening   C. Weekend   D. Weekday

24. If a 3.5% tax applied to the total cost of any call, what would be the TOTAL 24._____
cost of a 13-minute weekday, dial direct call to Golden, CO?
    A. $3.28   B. $3.39   C. $4.94   D. $6.39

25. What is the amount of discount from a dial direct, weekday call to 25._____
Tallahassee, FL cost as compared to a dial direct, weekend call to
Tallahassee?
    A. 45%   B. 30%   C. 60%   D. 20%

KEY (CORRECT ANSWERS)

1.	D		11.	C
2.	B		12.	D
3.	A		13.	A
4.	C		14.	C
5.	D		15.	A
6.	A		16.	D
7.	C		17.	A
8.	D		18.	B
9.	D		19.	C
10.	B		20.	B

    21. D
    22. D
    23. A
    24. B
    25. C

TEST 3

DIRECTIONS: Each question or incomplete statement is followed by several suggested answers or completions. Select the one that BEST answers the question or completes the statement. *PRINT THE LETTER OF THE CORRECT ANSWER IN THE SPACE AT THE RIGHT.*

Questions 1-7.

DIRECTIONS: Questions 1 through 7 are to be answered on the basis of the following graph.

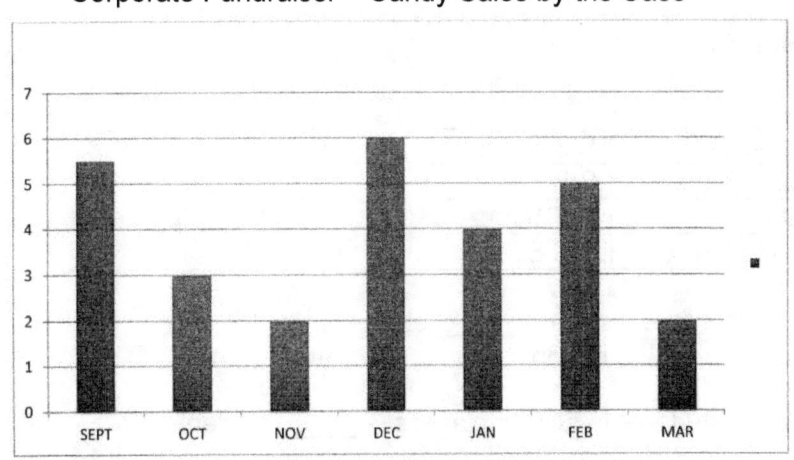

Corporate Fundraiser – Candy Sales by the Case

1. The vertical scale ranging from 0 to 7 represents the number of   1.____
   A. students selling candy
   B. candy sold in each case
   C. days each month that candy was sold
   D. cases of candy sold

2. Which two months had approximately the same amount of candy sold?   2.____
   A. November and March   B. September and February
   C. November and October   D. October and March

3. Which month showed a 100% increase in sales over the month of November?   3.____
   A. March   B. January   C. April   D. December

4. From month-to-month, which month saw an approximate 33% drop in sales from the previous month?   4.____
   A. March   B. September   C. January   D. October

5. The amount of candy sold in December is twice the amount of candy sold in which other month?   5.____
   A. October   B. March   C. January   D. September

6. What was the total amount of candy sold during the months shown on the graph?   6.____
   A. 44 cases   B. 35.5 cases   C. 23.5 cases   D. 27.5 cases

7. If the fundraiser extended the additional five months of the year and added   7.____
   an additional 65% in sales, approximately how many cases would be sold in
   total for an entire year?
   A. 40.5 cases   B. 37 cases   C. 45 cases   D. 27.5 cases

Questions 8-11.

DIRECTIONS: Questions 8 through 11 are to be answered on the basis of the following chart.

S = 10 students
s = 5 students

Mr. Hucklebee	S S S S s
Ms. Shopenhauer	S S S
Mr. White	S S S s
Mrs. Mulrooney	S S S

8. The size of Mr. White's class is _____ students.   8.____
   A. 30   B. 35   C. 40   D. 4

9. The total of all students in all four classes is _____ students.   9.____
   A. 150   B. 140   C. 125   D. 14

10. The average class size based on the above chart is _____ students.   10.____
    A. 140   B. 45   C. 35   D. 30

11. In order to ensure each teacher has the same amount of students in each   11.____
    class, how many students would need to transfer out of Mr. Hucklebee's class?
    A. 10
    B. 5
    C. 0
    d. 15 would need to transfer into his class

12. When alphabetized correctly, which of the following would be THIRD?   12.____
    A. box   B. departed   C. electrical   D. elemental

13. When alphabetized correctly, which of the following would be SECOND?   13.____
    A. polarize   B. omnipotent   C. polygraph   D. omniscient

14. When alphabetized correctly, which of the following would be THIRD?   14.____
    A. Macklemore, Jonathan   B. Mackelmore, J.
    C. DiCastro, Darian   D. Castro, Darren Henry

15. The group fought through the fog, *shambling* through the night, doing their best to stay upright.
    The word *shambling* means
    A. frozen in place
    B. running
    C. walking awkwardly
    D. shivering uncontrollably

    15._____

16. Many doctors agree that Gen-aspirin is the best for fighting headaches. It comes in different flavors and is easy to swallow.
    Is this a valid or invalid argument?
    A. Invalid
    B. Valid

    16._____

Questions 17-21.

DIRECTIONS: Questions 17 through 21 are to be answered on the basis of the following paragraph.

Hospital workers and volunteers often ask Mr. Ansley to educate children who are hospitalized with primary ciliary dyskinesia (PCD). As he goes through the precautionary cleaning process (scrubbing, donning sterilized clothes, etc.) in order to see his students, Mr. Ansley wonders why their parents add the stress and pressure of schooling and trying to play catch-up because of the amount of time spent in the hospital and not in the classroom, which is an unfortunate side effect of patients with PCD. These children go through so many painful treatments on a given day that it seems punishing to subject them to schooling as normal children do, especially with life expectancy being as short as it is.

17. What is meant by *precautionary* in the second sentence?
    A. Careful   B. Protective   C. Sterilizing   D. Medical

    17._____

18. What is the MAIN idea of this passage?
    A. The preparation to visit a patient with primary ciliary dyskinesia is extensive.
    B. Children with PCD are unable to live normal lives.
    C. Children with PCD die young.
    D. Certain allowances should be made for children with PCD.

    18._____

19. What is the author's purpose?
    A. To advise
    B. To educate
    C. To establish credibility
    D. To amuse

    19._____

20. What is the author's tone?
    A. Cruel
    B. Sympathetic
    C. Disbelieving
    D. Cheerful

    20._____

21. How is Mr. Ansley so familiar with the procedures used when visiting a child with PCD?
    A. He has read about it
    B. He works in the hospital.
    C. His child has PCD.
    D. He tutors them on a regular basis.

    21._____

Questions 22-25.

DIRECTIONS: One of the underlined words in Questions 22 through 25 should be changed. Select the one that should be changed and print the letter of the word that would change the underlined word.

22. After we washed the fruit that had growing in the garden, we knew there was a store that would buy them.
    A. washing   B. grown   C. is   D. No change

23. When the temperature drops under 32 degrees (F), the water on the lake freezes, which allowed children to skate across it.
    A. dropped   B. froze   C. allows   D. No change

24. My friend's bulldog, while chasing cars in the street, always manages to knock over our garbage bins.
    A. chased   B. manage   C. knocks   D. No change

25. Some of the ice on the driveway has melted.
    A. having melted   B. have melted
    C. has melt   D. No change

KEY (CORRECT ANSWERS)

1.	D		11.	A
2.	A		12.	C
3.	B		13.	D
4.	C		14.	B
5.	A		15.	C
6.	D		16.	A
7.	C		17.	C
8.	B		18.	D
9.	B		19.	A
10.	C		20.	B

21.	D
22.	B
23.	C
24.	D
25.	D

TEST 4

DIRECTIONS: Each question or incomplete statement is followed by several suggested answers or completions. Select the one that BEST answers the question or completes the statement. *PRINT THE LETTER OF THE CORRECT ANSWER IN THE SPACE AT THE RIGHT.*

Questions 1-2.

DIRECTIONS: One of the underlined words in Questions 1 and 2 should be changed. Select the one that should be changed and print the letter of the word that would change the underlined word.

1. You can get to Martha's Vineyard by driving from Boston to Woods Hole. Once there, you can travel over on a boat, but you may find traveling by airplane to be more exciting.
    A. they   B. visitors   C. it   D. No change   1.____

2. When John wants to go to the store looking for milk and eggs, you must remember to bring his wallet.
    A. them   B. he   C. its   D. No change   2.____

3. An item that sells for $400 is put on sale at $145. What is the percentage of decrease?
    A. 25%   B. 28%   C. 64%   D. 36%   3.____

4. Two Junior College Mathematics courses have a total of 510 students. The 9:00 AM class has 60 more than the 12:30 PM class. How many students are in the 12:30 class?
    A. 225   B. 285   C. 255   D. 205   4.____

5. If a car gets 26 miles per gallon and it has driven 75,210 miles, approximately what is the number of gallons of gas that it has used?
    A. 3,000   B. 2,585   C. 165   D. 1,800   5.____

6. Which one of the following sentences about proper telephone usage is NOT always correct? When answering a telephone, you should
    A. know who you are speaking to
    B. give the caller your undivided attention
    C. identify yourself to the caller
    D. obtain the information your caller wishes before you do other work   6.____

7. You are part of the "Safety at Work" committee, which is dedicated to ensuring safety of employees. During your regular shift, you notice an employee in violation of one of your committee's rules. Which of the following actions should you take FIRST?
   A. Speak with the employee about the safety rules and mandate them to stop breaking the rules.
   B. Speak to the employee about safety rules and point out the rule they violated.
   C. Bring up the issue during the next committee meeting.
   D. Report the violation to the employee's superiors.

8. Part of your duties is overseeing employee confidential information. A friend and coworker of yours asks to obtain information concerning another employee. Which is the BEST action to take?
   A. Ask the coworker if you can share the information.
   B. Ask your supervisor if you can give the information to your friend.
   C. Refuse to give the information to your friend.
   D. Give the information to your friend.

9. Which of the following words means the OPPOSITE of protract?
   A. Extend   B. Hesitant   C. Curtail   D. Plethora

10. Which of the following words means the OPPOSITE of conserve?
    A. Relinquish   B. Waste   C. Proficient   D. Rigid

11. Which of the following words means the SAME as dissipate?
    A. Scatter   B. Emancipate
    C. Engage   D. Accumulate

12. Your office just purchased 14 fax machines. Each fax machine costs $79.99. How much did the 14 fax machines cost?
    A. $1,119.86   B. $1,108.77   C. $1,201.44   D. $1,788.22

Questions 13-19.

DIRECTIONS: Questions 13 through 19 are to be answered on the basis of the following chart.

Office City	Sales Rank	Production Materials Produced	Rank for Production	Damaged Materials	Employees	Percent of Profit	Sales Points	Weeks Without Injuries
Springfield	13.6	271	12	1	34	35	36	7
Philadelphia	17	274	4	3	25	41	20	4
Gary	16	260	10	5	34	34	21	3
Boulder	5	10	6	9	38	15	20	8
Miami	81	3	81	77	133	4	2	0
Houston	2	370	2	0	95	66	100	16
Battle Creek	82	290	82	81	91	13	9	2

13. Between Philadelphia and Battle Creek, how many damaged materials were there?   13.____
    A. 84   B. 78   C. 45   D. 86

14. How many offices have had 5 or more weeks without injuries?   14.____
    A. 3   B. 4   C. 2   D. 0

15. What was the TOTAL number of damaged materials for the offices in Boulder, Miami, Houston, and Springfield offices?   15.____
    A. 91   B. 87   C. 80   D. 77

16. What were the TOTAL sales points of Houston, Battle Creek, and Gary?   16.____
    A. 115   B. 145   C. 160   D. 130

17. Which of the offices had the LOWEST number of weeks without an injury?   17.____
    A. Battle Creek   B. Miami   C. Gary   D. Philadelphia

18. If worker efficiency is a percentage based on the number of workers at an office and the amount of materials produced, which office has the GREATEST worker efficiency?   18.____
    A. Philadelphia   B. Springfield   C. Boulder   D. Gary

19. If the company was looking to close a facility, which of the following factors would NOT be a reason to close the Miami office?   19.____
    A. Weeks without injury   B. Sales rank
    C. Production materials produced   D. Employees

Questions 20-25.

DIRECTIONS: In answering Questions 20 through 25, select the sentence in which the underlined word is used correctly.

20. A. Jon needs to increase his capitol by 30% to invest in my business.   20.____
    B. The organization is reevaluating it's decision to purchase the building.
    C. The office supply store sells computer paper and stationery.
    D. The quarterback and running back left there helmets on the bus.

21. A. The police sergeant sited me for disorderly conduct and driving without a license.   21.____
    B. The votes have already been counted.
    C. The professor's theory contradicts the principals of Einstein and Newton.
    D. Who's glass of water is on the table?

22. A. The board of trustees decided to accept the CEO's resignation.   22.____
    B. Lose hats will help keep your head from hurting.
    C. She complemented me on my exquisite dinner tastes.
    D. Jamaal offered him some sound advise.

23. A. In class today, Maya lead us in the reciting of the pledge.
    B. Doctors worry about the affects of drinking red wine right before bed.
    C. The workers used sledge hammers to break up the pavement.
    D. The teacher gave her students wise council.

    23.____

24. A. This building was formerly the site of one of the city's oldest department stores.
    B. In his position, Albert must be very discrete in handling confidential information.
    C. He was to tired to continue the race.
    D. Each of his mortgage payments as about evenly divided between principle and interest.

    24.____

25. A. The police spent several hours at the cite of the accident.
    B. A majority of the public support capitol punishment.
    C. The magician used mirrors to create a convincing illusion.
    D. The heiress flouted her wealth by wearing expensive jewelry.

    25.____

KEY (CORRECT ANSWERS)

1.	D		11.	A
2.	B		12.	A
3.	C		13.	A
4.	A		14.	A
5.	A		15.	B
6.	D		16.	D
7.	B		17.	B
8.	C		18.	A
9.	C		19.	D
10.	B		20.	C

21. B
22. A
23. C
24. A
25. C

CLERICAL ABILITIES
EXAMINATION SECTION
TEST 1

DIRECTIONS: Each question or incomplete statement is followed by several suggested answers or completions. Select the one that BEST answers the question or completes the statement. *PRINT THE LETTER OF THE CORRECT ANSWER IN THE SPACE AT THE RIGHT.*

Questions 1-4.

DIRECTIONS: Questions 1 through 4 are to be answered on the basis of the information given below.

    The most commonly used filing system and the one that is easiest to learn is alphabetical filing. This involves putting records in an A to Z order, according to the letters of the alphabet. The name of a person is filed by using the following order: first, the surname or last name; second, the first name; third, the middle name or middle initial. For example, *Henry C. Young* is filed under *Y* and thereafter under *Young, Henry C.* The name of a company is filed in the same way. For example, *Long Cabinet Co.* is filed under *L* while *John T. Long Cabinet Co.* is filed under *L* and thereafter under *Long, John T. Cabinet Co.*

1. The one of the following which lists the names of persons in the CORRECT alphabetical order is:
   A. Mary Carrie, Helen Carrol, James Carson, John Carter
   B. James Carson, Mary Carrie, John Carter, Helen Carrol
   C. Helen Carrol, James Carson, John Carter, Mary Carrie
   D. John Carter, Helen Carrol, Mary Carrie, James Carson

   1.____

2. The one of the following which lists the names of persons in the CORRECT alphabetical order is:
   A. Jones, John C.; Jones, John A.; Jones, John P.; Jones, John K.
   B. Jones, John P.; Jones, John K.; Jones, John C.; Jones, John A.
   C. Jones, John A.; Jones, John C.; Jones, John K.; Jones, John P.
   D. Jones, John K.; Jones, John C.; Jones, John A.; Jones, John P.

   2.____

3. The one of the following which lists the names of the companies in the CORRECT alphabetical order is:
   A. Blane Co., Blake Co., Block Co., Blear Co.
   B. Blake Co., Blane Co., Blear Co., Block Co.
   C. Block Co., Blear Co., Blane Co., Blake Co.
   D. Blear Co., Blake Co., Blane Co., Block Co.

   3.____

4. You are to return to the file an index card on *Barry C. Wayne Materials and Supplies Co.*
   Of the following, the CORRECT alphabetical group that you should return the index card to is
   A. A to G   B. H to M   C. N to S   D. T to Z

4._____

Questions 5-10.

DIRECTIONS: In each of Questions 5 through 10, the names of four people are given. For each question, choose as your answer the one of the four names given which should be filed FIRST according to the usual system of alphabetical filing of names, as described in the following paragraph.

In filing names, you must start with the last name. Names are filed in order of the first letter of the last name, then the second letter, etc. Therefore, BAILY would be filed before BROWN, which would be filed before COLT. A name with fewer letters of the same type comes first, i.e., Smith before Smithe. If the last names are the same, the names are filed alphabetically by the first name. If the first name is an initial, a name with an initial would come before a first name that starts with the same letter as the initial. Therefore, I. BROWN would come before IRA BROWN. Finally, if both last name and first name are the same, the name would be filed alphabetically by the middle name, once again an initial coming before a middle name which starts with the same letter as the initial. If there is no middle name at all, the name would come before those with middle initials or names.

SAMPLE QUESTION: A. Lester Daniels
                  B. William Dancer
                  C. Nathan Danzig
                  D. Dan Lester

The last names beginning with D are filed before the last name beginning with L. Since DANIELS, DANCER, and DANZIG all begin with the same three letters, you must look at the fourth letter of the last name to determine which name should be filed first. C comes before I or Z in the alphabet, so DANCER is filed before DANIELS or DANZIG. Therefore, the answer to the above sample question is B.

5. A. Scott Biala
   B. Mary Byala
   C. Martin Baylor
   D. Francis Bauer

5._____

6. A. Howard J. Black
   B. Howard Black
   C. J. Howard Black
   D. John H. Black

6._____

7. A. Theodora Garth Kingston
   B. Theadore Barth Kingston
   C. Thomas Kingston
   D. Thomas T. Kingston

7._____

8. A. Paulette Mary Huerta
    B. Paul M. Huerta
    C. Paulette L. Huerta
    D. Peter A. Huerta

9. A. Martha Hunt Morgan
    B. Martin Hunt Morgan
    C. Mary H. Morgan
    D. Martine H. Morgan

10. A. James T. Meerschaum
    B. James M. Mershum
    C. James F. Mearshaum
    D. James N. Meshum

Questions 11-14.

DIRECTIONS: Questions 11 through 14 are to be answered SOLELY on the basis of the following information.

You are required to file various documents in file drawers which are labeled according to the following pattern:

DOCUMENTS

MEMOS		LETTERS	
File	Subject	File	Subject
84PM1	(A-L)	84PC1	(A-L)
84PM2	(M-Z)	84PC2	(M-Z)

REPORTS		INQUIRIES	
File	Subject	File	Subject
84PR1	(A-L)	84PQ1	(A-L)
84PR2	(M-Z)	84PQ2	(M-Z)

11. A letter dealing with a burglary should be filed in the drawer labeled
    A. 84PM1   B. 84PC1   C. 84PR1   D. 84PQ2

12. A report on Statistics should be found in the drawer labeled
    A. 84PM1   B. 84PC2   C. 84PR2   D. 84PQS

13. An inquiry is received about parade permit procedures. It should be filed in the drawer labeled
    A. 84PM2   B. 84PC1   C. 84PR1   D. 84PQ2

14. A police officer has a question about a robbery report you filed. You should pull this file from the drawer labeled
    A. 84PM1   B. 84PM2   C. 84PR1   D. 84PR2

Questions 15-22.

DIRECTIONS: Each of Questions 15 through 22 consists of four or six numbered names. For each question, choose the option (A, B, C, or D) which indicates the order in which the names should be filed in accordance with the following filing instructions:
- File alphabetically according to last name, then first name, then middle initial.
- File according to each successive letter within a name.
- When comparing two names in which the letters in the longer name are identical to the corresponding letters in the shorter name, the shorter name is filed first.
- When the last names are the same, initials are always filed before names beginning with the same letter.

15. I. Ralph Robinson
    II. Alfred Ross
    III. Luis Robles
    IV. James Roberts

    The CORRECT filing sequence for the above names should be
    A. IV, II, I, III   B. I, IV, III, II   C. III, IV, I, II   D. IV, I, III, II

16. I. Irwin Goodwin
    II. Inez Gonzalez
    III. Irene Goodman
    IV. Ira S. Goodwin
    V. Ruth I. Goldstein
    VI. M.B. Goodman

    The CORRECT filing sequence for the above names should be
    A. V, II, I, IV, III, VI   B. V, II, VI, III, IV, I
    C. V, II, III, VI, IV, I   D. V, II, III, VI, I, IV

17. I. George Allan
    II. Gregory Allen
    III. Gary Allen
    IV. George Allen

    The CORRECT filing sequence for the above names should be
    A. IV, III, I, II   B. I, IV, II, III   C. III, IV, I, II   D. I, III, IV, II

18. I. Simon Kauffman
    II. Leo Kaufman
    III. Robert Kaufmann
    IV. Paul Kauffmann

    The CORRECT filing sequence for the above names should be
    A. I, IV, II, III   B. II, IV, III, I   C. III, II, IV, I   D. I, II, III, IV

19. I. Roberta Williams
    II. Robin Wilson
    III. Roberta Wilson
    IV. Robin Williams

    The CORRECT filing sequence for the above names should be
    A. III, II, IV, I   B. I, IV, III, II   C. I, II, III, IV   D. III, I, II, IV

20. I. Lawrence Shultz
    II. Albert Schultz
    III. Theodore Schwartz
    IV. Thomas Schwarz
    V. Alvin Schultz
    VI. Leonard Shultz

    The CORRECT filing sequence for the above names should be
    A. II, V, III, IV, I, VI   B. IV, III, V, I, II, VI
    C. II, V, I, VI, III, IV   D. I, VI, II, V, III, IV

21. I. McArdle
    II. Mayer
    III. Maletz
    IV. McNiff
    V. Meyer
    VI. MacMahon

    The CORRECT filing sequence for the above names should be
    A. I, IV, VI, III, II, V   B. II, I, IV, VI, III, V
    C. VI, III, II, I, IV, V   D. VI, III, II, V, I, IV

22. I. Jack E. Johnson
    II. R.H. Jackson
    III. Bertha Jackson
    IV. J.T. Johnson
    V. Ann Johns
    VI. John Jacobs

    The CORRECT filing sequence for the above names should be
    A. II, III, VI, V, IV, I   B. III, II, VI, V, IV, I
    C. VI, II, III, I, V, IV   D. III, II, VI, IV, V, I

Questions 23-30.

DIRECTIONS: The code table below shows 10 letters with matching numbers. For each question, there are three sets of letters. Each set of letters is followed by a set of numbers which may or may not match their correct letter according to the code table. For each question, check all three sets of letters and numbers and mark your answer:
- A. if no pairs are correctly matched
- B. if only one pair is correctly matched
- C. if only two pairs are correctly matched
- D. if all three pairs are correctly matched

CODE TABLE

T	M	V	D	S	P	R	G	B	H
1	2	3	4	5	6	7	8	9	0

SAMPLE QUESTION: TMVDSP – 123456
RGBHTM – 789011
DSPRGB – 256789

In the sample question above, the first set of numbers correctly match its set of letters. But the second and third pairs contain mistakes. In the second pair, M is correctly matched with number 1. According to the code table, letter M should be correctly matched with number 2. In the third pair, the letter D is incorrectly matched with number 2. According to the code table, letter D should be correctly matched with number 4. Since only one of the pairs is correctly matched, the answer to this sample question is B.

23. RSBMRM – 759262
    GDSRVH – 845730
    VDBRTM - 349713

24. TGVSDR – 183247
    SMHRDP – 520647
    TRMHSR - 172057

25. DSPRGM – 456782
    MVDBHT – 234902
    HPMDBT - 062491

26. BVPTRD – 936184
    GDPHMB – 807029
    GMRHMV - 827032

27. MGVRSH – 283750
    TRDMBS – 174295
    SPRMGV - 567283

23.____

24.____

25.____

26.____

27.____

28. SGBSDM – 489542   28.____
    MGHPTM – 290612
    MPBMHT - 269301

29. TDPBHM – 146902   29.____
    VPBMRS – 369275
    GDMBHM - 842902

30. MVPTBV – 236194   30.____
    PDRTMB – 47128
    BGTMSM - 981232

KEY (CORRECT ANSWERS)

1.	A	11.	B	21.	C
2.	C	12.	C	22.	B
3.	B	13.	D	23.	B
4.	D	14.	D	24.	B
5.	D	15.	D	25.	C
6.	B	16.	C	26.	A
7.	B	17.	D	27.	D
8.	B	18.	A	28.	A
9.	A	19.	B	29.	D
10.	C	20.	A	30.	A

TEST 2

DIRECTIONS: Each question or incomplete statement is followed by several suggested answers or completions. Select the one that BEST answers the question or completes the statement. *PRINT THE LETTER OF THE CORRECT ANSWER IN THE SPACE AT THE RIGHT.*

Questions 1-10.

DIRECTIONS: Questions 1 through 10 each consists of two columns, each containing four lines of names, numbers and/or addresses. For each question, compare the lines in Column I with the lines in Column II to see if they match exactly, and mark your answer A, B, C, or D, according to the following instructions:
    A. all four lines match exactly
    B. only three lines match exactly
    C. only two lines match exactly
    D. only one line matches exactly

    COLUMN I   COLUMN II

1.   I.   Earl Hodgson   Earl Hodgson   1.____
    II.   1409870   1408970
    III.   Shore Ave.   Schore Ave.
    IV.   Macon Rd.   Macon Rd.

2.   I.   9671485   9671485   2.____
    II.   470 Astor Court   470 Astor Court
    III.   Halprin, Phillip   Halperin, Phillip
    IV.   Frank D. Poliseo   Frank D. Poliseo

3.   I.   Tandem Associates   Tandom Associates   3.____
    II.   144-17 Northern Blvd.   144-17 Northern Blvd.
    III.   Alberta Forchi   Albert Forchi
    IV.   Kings Park, NY 10751   Kings Point, NY 10751

4.   I.   Bertha C. McCormack   Bertha C. McCormack   4.____
    II.   Clayton, MO   Clayton, MO
    III.   976-4242   976-4242
    IV.   New City, NY 10951   New City, NY 10951

5.   I.   George C. Morill   George C. Morrill   5.____
    II.   Columbia, SC 29201   Columbia, SD 29201
    III.   Louis Ingham   Louis Ingham
    IV.   3406 Forest Ave.   3406 Forest Ave.

6.   I.   506 S. Elliott Pl.   506 S. Elliott Pl.   6.____
    II.   Herbert Hall   Hurbert Hall
    III.   4712 Rockaway Pkway   4712 Rockaway Pkway
    IV.   169 E. 7 St.   169 E. 7 St.

7. I.   345 Park Ave.   345 Park Pl.   7.____
    II. Colman Oven Corp.   Coleman Oven Corp.
    III. Robert Conte   Robert Conti
    IV. 6179846   6179846

8. I.   Grigori Schierber   Grigori Schierber   8.____
    II. Des Moines, Iowa   Des Moines, Iowa
    III. Gouverneur Hospital   Gouverneur Hospital
    IV. 91-35 Cresskill Pl.   91-35 Cresskill Pl.

9. I.   Jeffery Janssen   Jeffrey Janssen   9.____
    II. 8041071   8041071
    III. 40 Rockefeller Plaza   40 Rockafeller Plaza
    IV. 407 6 St.   406 7 St.

10. I.   5971996   5871996   10.____
    II. 3113 Knickerbocker Ave. 31123 Knickerbocker Ave.
    III. 8434 Boston Post Rd.   8424 Boston Post Rd.
    IV. Penn Station   Penn Station

Questions 11-14.

DIRECTIONS: Questions 11 through 14 are to be answered by looking at the four groups of names and addresses listed below (I, II, III, and IV), and then finding out the number of groups that have their corresponding numbered lies exactly the same.

	GROUP I	GROUP II
Line 1.	Richmond General Hospital	Richman General Hospital
Line 2.	Geriatric Clinic	Geriatric Clinic
Line 3.	3975 Paerdegat St.	3975 Peardegat St.
Line 4.	Loudonville, New York 11538	Londonville, New York 11538

	GROUP III	GROUP IV
Line 1.	Richmond General Hospital	Richmend General Hospital
Line 2.	Geriatric Clinic	Geriatric Clinic
Line 3.	3795 Paerdegat St.	3975 Paerdegat St.
Line 4.	Loudonville, New York 11358	Loudonville, New York 11538

1. In how many groups is line one exactly the same?   11.____
    A. Two   B. Three   C. Four   D. None

12. In how many groups is line two exactly the same?   12.____
    A. Two   B. Three   C. Four   D. None

13. In how many groups is line three exactly the same?   13.____
    A. Two   B. Three   C. Four   D. None

14. In how many groups is line four exactly the same?   14._____
    A. Two   B. Three   C. Four   D. None

Questions 15-18.

DIRECTIONS: Each of Questions 15 through 18 has two lists of names and addresses. Each list contains three sets of names and addresses. Check each of the three sets in the list on the right to see if they are the same as the corresponding set in the list on the left. Mark your answers:
   A. if none of the sets in the right list are the same as those in the left list
   B. if only one of the sets in the right list is the same as those in the left list
   C. if only two of the sets in the right list are the same as those in the left list
   D. if all three sets in the right list are the same as those in the left list

15. Mary T. Berlinger   Mary T. Berlinger   15._____
    2351 Hampton St.   2351 Hampton St.
    Monsey, N.Y. 20117   Monsey, N.Y. 20117

    Eduardo Benes   Eduardo Benes
    483 Kingston Avenue   473 Kingston Avenue
    Central Islip, N.Y. 11734   Central Islip, N.Y. 11734

    Alan Carrington Fuchs   Alan Carrington Fuchs
    17 Gnarled Hollow Road   17 Gnarled Hollow Road
    Los Angeles, CA 91635   Los Angeles, CA 91685

16. David John Jacobson   David John Jacobson   16._____
    178 34 St. Apt. 4C   178 53 St. Apt. 4C
    New York, N.Y. 00927   New York, N.Y. 00927

    Ann-Marie Calonella   Ann-Marie Calonella
    7243 South Ridge Blvd.   7243 South Ridge Blvd.
    Bakersfield, CA 96714   Bakersfield, CA 96714

    Pauline M. Thompson   Pauline M. Thomson
    872 Linden Ave.   872 Linden Ave.
    Houston, Texas 70321   Houston, Texas 70321

17. Chester LeRoy Masterton   Chester LeRoy Masterson   17._____
    152 Lacy Rd.   152 Lacy Rd.
    Kankakee, Ill. 54532   Kankakee, Ill. 54532

    William Maloney   William Maloney
    S. LaCrosse Pla.   S. LaCross Pla.
    Wausau, Wisconsin 52136   Wausau, Wisconsin 52146

    Cynthia V. Barnes   Cynthia V. Barnes
    16 Pines Rd.   16 Pines Rd.
    Greenpoint, Miss. 20376   Greenpoint,, Miss. 20376

4 (#2)

18. Marcel Jean Frontenac   Marcel Jean Frontenac   18._____
     8 Burton On The Water   6 Burton On The Water
     Calender, Me. 01471   Calender, Me. 01471

     J. Scott Marsden   J. Scott Marsden
     174 S. Tipton St.   174 Tipton St.
     Cleveland, Ohio   Cleveland, Ohio

     Lawrence T. Haney   Lawrence T. Haney
     171 McDonough St.   171 McDonough St.
     Decatur, Ga. 31304   Decatur, Ga. 31304

Questions 19-26.

DIRECTIONS: Each of Questions 19 through 26 has two lists of numbers. Each list contains three sets of numbers. Check each of the three sets in the list on the right to see if they are the same as the corresponding set in the list on the left. Mark your answers:
    A. if none of the sets in the right list are the same as those in the left list
    B. if only one of the sets in the right list is the same as those in the left list
    C. if only two of the sets in the right list are the same as those in the left list
    D. if all three sets in the right list are the same as those in the left lists

19. 7354183476   7354983476   19._____
     4474747744   4474747774
     5791430231   57914302311

20. 7143592185   7143892185   20._____
     8344517699   8344518699
     9178531263   9178531263

21. 2572114731   257214731   21._____
     8806835476   8806835476
     8255831246   8255831246

22. 331476853821   331476858621   22._____
     6976658532996   6976655832996
     3766042113715   3766042113745

23. 8806663315   88066633115   23._____
     74477138449   74477138449
     211756663666   211756663666

24. 990006966996   99000696996   24._____
     53022219743   53022219843
     4171171117717   4171171177717

25. 24400222433004   24400222433004   25._____
     5300030055000355   5300030055500355
     20000075532002022   20000075532002022

26. 611166640660001116   61116664066001116   26._____
     7111300117001100733   7111300117001100733
     26666446664476518   26666446664476518

Questions 27-30.

DIRECTIONS: Questions 27 through 30 are to be answered by picking the answer which is in the correct numerical order, from the lowest number to the highest number, in each question.

27. A. 44533, 44518, 44516, 44547   27._____
    B. 44516, 44518, 44533, 44547
    C. 44547, 44533, 44518, 44516
    D. 44518, 44516, 44547, 44533

28. A. 95587, 95593, 95601, 95620   28._____
    B. 95601, 95620, 95587, 95593
    C. 95593, 95587, 95601. 95620
    D. 95620, 95601, 95593, 95587

29. A. 232212, 232208, 232232, 232223   29._____
    B. 232208, 232223, 232212, 232232
    C. 232208, 232212, 232223, 232232
    D. 232223, 232232, 232208, 232208

30. A. 113419, 113521, 113462, 113462   30._____
    B. 113588, 113462, 113521, 113419
    C. 113521, 113588, 113419, 113462
    D. 113419, 113462, 113521, 113588

KEY (CORRECT ANSWERS)

1.	C	11.	A	21.	C
2.	B	12.	C	22.	A
3.	D	13.	A	23.	D
4.	A	14.	A	24.	A
5.	C	15.	C	25.	C
6.	B	16.	B	26.	C
7.	D	17.	B	27.	B
8.	A	18.	B	28.	A
9.	D	19.	B	29.	C
10.	C	20.	B	30.	D

CODING

EXAMINATION SECTION

COMMENTARY

An ingenious question-type called coding, involving elements of alphabetizing, filing, name and number comparison, and evaluative judgment and application, has currently won wide acceptance in testing circles for measuring clerical aptitude and general ability, particularly on the senior (middle) grades (levels).

While the directions for this question usually vary in detail, the candidate is generally asked to consider groups of names, codes, and numbers, and then, according to a given plan, to arrange codes in alphabetic order; to arrange these in numerical sequence; to re-arrange columns of names and numbers in correct order; to espy errors in coding; to choose the correct coding arrangement in consonance with the given directions and examples, etc.

This question-type appear to have few parameters in respect to form, substance, or degree of difficulty.

Accordingly, acquaintance with, and practice in, the coding question is recommended for the serious candidate.

TEST 1

DIRECTIONS: Questions 1 through 8 are to be answered on the basis of the code table and the instructions given below.

Code Letter for Traffic Problem	B	H	Q	J	F	L	M	I
Code Number for Action Taken	1	2	3	4	5	6	7	8

Assume that each of the capital letters on the above chart is a radio code for a particular traffic problem and that the number immediately below each capital letter is the radio code for the correct action to be taken to deal with the problem. For instance, "1" is the action to be taken to deal with problem "B", "2" is the action to be taken to deal with problem "H", and so forth.

In each question, a series of code letters is given in Column 1. Column 2 gives four different arrangements of code numbers. You are to pick the answer (A, B, C, or D) in Column 2 that gives the code numbers that match the code letters in the same order.

SAMPLE QUESTION

Column 1
BHLFMQ

Column 2
A. 125678
B. 216573
C. 127653
D. 126573

According to the chart, the code numbers that correspond to these code letters are as follows: B – 1, M – 2, L – 6, F – 5, M – 7, Q – 3. Therefore, the right answer is 126573. This answer is D in Column 2.

2 (#1)

	Column 1	Column 2	

1. BHQLMI
   - A. 123456
   - B. 123567
   - C. 123678
   - D. 125678

   1.____

2. HBJQLF
   - A. 214365
   - B. 213456
   - C. 213465
   - D. 214387

   2.____

3. QHMLFJ
   - A. 321654
   - B. 345678
   - C. 327645
   - D. 327654

   3.____

4. FLQJIM
   - A. 543287
   - B. 563487
   - C. 564378
   - D. 654378

   4.____

5. FBIHMJ
   - A. 518274
   - B. 152874
   - C. 528164
   - D. 517842

   5.____

6. MIHFQB
   - A. 872341
   - B. 782531
   - C. 782341
   - D. 783214

   6.____

7. JLFHQIM
   - A. 465237
   - B. 456387
   - C. 4652387
   - D. 4562387

   7.____

8. LBJQIFH
   - A. 614382
   - B. 6134852
   - C. 61437852
   - D. 61431852

   8.____

KEY (CORRECT ANSWERS)

1. C
2. A
3. D
4. B
5. A
6. B
7. C
8. A

TEST 2

DIRECTIONS: Each question or incomplete statement is followed by several suggested answers or completions. Select the one that BEST answers the question or completes the statement. *PRINT THE LETTER OF THE CORRECT ANSWER IN THE SPACE AT THE RIGHT.*

Questions 1-5.

DIRECTIONS: Questions 1 through 5 are based on the following list showing the name and number of each of nine inmates.

    1. Johnson   4. Thompson   7. Gordon
    2. Smith   5. Frank   8. Porter
    3. Edwards   6. Murray   9. Lopez

Each question consists of 3 sets of numbers and letters. Each set should consist of the numbers of three inmates and the first letter of each of their names. The letters should be in the same order as the numbers. In at least two of the three choices, there will be an error. On your answer sheet, mark only that choice in which the letters correspond with the numbers and are in the same order. If all three sets are wrong, mark choice D in your answer space.

SAMPLE QUESTION
    A. 386 EPM
    B. 542 FST
    C. 474 LGT

Since 3 corresponds to E for Edwards, 8 corresponds to P for Porter, and 6 corresponds to M for Murray, choice A is correct and should be entered in your answer space. Choice B is wrong because letters T and S have been reversed. Choice C is wrong because the first number, which is 4, does NOT correspond with the first letter of choice C, which is L. It should have been T. If choice A were also wrong, then D would be the correct answer.

1. A. 382 EGS   B. 461 TMJ   C. 875 PLF   1.____

2. A. 549 FLT   B. 692 MJS   C. 758 GSP   2.____

3. A. 936 LEM   B. 253 FSE   C. 147 JTL   3.____

4. A. 569 PML   B. 716 GJP   C. 842 PTS   4.____

5. A. 356 FEM   B. 198 JPL   C. 637 MEG   5.____

Questions 6-10.

DIRECTIONS: Questions 6 through 10 are to be answered on the basis of the following information:

In order to make sure stock is properly located, incoming units are stored as follows:

STOCK NUMBERS	BIN NUMBERS
00100 – 39999	D30, L44
40000 – 69999	14L, D38
70000 – 99999	41L, 80D
100000 and over	614, 83D

Using the above table, choose the answer A, B, C, or D, which lists the correct Bin Number for the Stock Number given.

6. 17243
   A. 41L   B. 83D   C. 14L   D. D30

7. 9219
   A. D38   B. L44   C. 614   D. 41L

8. 90125
   A. 41L   B. 614   C. D38   D. D30

9. 10001
   A. L44   B. D38   C. 80D   D. 83D

10. 200100
    A. 41L   B. 14L   C. 83D   D. D30

KEY (CORRECT ANSWERS)

1. B   6. D
2. D   7. B
3. A   8. A
4. C   9. A
5. C   10. C

TEST 3

DIRECTIONS: Each question or incomplete statement is followed by several suggested answers or completions. Select the one that BEST answers the question or completes the statement. *PRINT THE LETTER OF THE CORRECT ANSWER IN THE SPACE AT THE RIGHT.*

Questions 1-9.

DIRECTIONS: Assume that the Police Department is planning to conduct a statistical study of individuals who have been convicted of crimes during a certain year. For the purpose of this study, identification numbers are being assigned to individuals in the following manner:

The first two digits indicate the age of the individual.
The third digit indicates the sex of the individual:
    1. Male
    2. Female
The fourth digit indicates the type of crime involved:
    1. criminal homicide
    2. forcible rape
    3. robbery
    4. aggravated assault
    5. burglary
    6. larceny
    7. auto theft
    8. other
The fifth and sixth digits indicate the month in which the conviction occurred:
    01.   January
    02.   February, etc.

Questions 1 through 9 are to be answered SOLELY on the basis of the above information and the following list of individuals and identification numbers.

Name	Number	Name	Number
Abbott, Richard	271304	Morris, Chris	212705
Collins, Terry	352111	Owens, William	231412
Elders, Edward	191207	Parker, Leonard	291807
George, Linda	182809	Robinson, Charles	311102
Hill, Leslie	251702	Sands, Jean	202610
Jones, Jackie	301106	Smith, Michael	42108
Lewis, Edith	402406	Turner, Donald	191601
Mack, Helen	332509	White, Barbara	242803

1. The number of women on the above list is   1.____
   A. 6   B. 7   C. 8   D. 9

2. The two convictions which occurred during February were for the crimes of
   A. aggravated assault and auto theft
   B. auto theft and criminal homicide
   C. burglary and larceny
   D. forcible rape and robbery

3. The ONLY man convicted of auto theft was
   A. Richard Abbott
   B. Leslie Hill
   C. Chris Morris
   D. Leonard Parker

4. The number of people on the list who were 25 years old or older is
   A. 6   B. 7   C. 8   D. 9

5. The OLDEST person on the list is
   A. Terry Collins
   B. Edith Lewis
   C. Helen Mack
   D. Michael Smith

6. The two people on the list who are the same age are
   A. Richard Abbott and Michael Smith
   B. Edward Elders and Donald Turner
   C. Linda George and Helen Mack
   D. Leslie Hill and Charles Robinson

7. A 28-year-old man who was convicted of aggravated assault in October would have identification number
   A. 281410   B. 281509   C. 282311   D. 282409

8. A 33-year-old woman convicted in April of criminal homicide would have identification number
   A. 331140   B. 331204   C. 332014   D. 332104

9. The number of people on the above list who were convicted during the first six months of the year is
   A. 6   B. 7   C. 8   D. 9

Questions 10-19.

DIRECTIONS: The following is a list of patients who were referred by various clinics to the laboratory for tests. After each name is a patient identification number. Questions 10 through 19 are to be answered on the basis of the information contained in this list and the explanation accompanying it.

The first digit refers to the clinic which made the referral:
1. cardiac
2. Renal
3. Pediatrics
4. Ophthalmology
5. Orthopedics
6. Hematology
7. Gynecology
8. Neurology
9. Gastroenterology

The second digit refers to the sex of the patient:
1. male
2. female

The third and fourth digits give the age of the patient
The last two digits give the day of the month the laboratory tests were performed

LABORATORY REFERRALS DURING JANUARY

Adams, Jacqueline	320917	Miller, Michael	511806
Black, Leslie	813406	Pratt, William	214411
Cook, Marie	511616	Rogers, Ellen	722428
Fisher, Pat	914625	Saunders, Sally	310229
Jackson, Lee	923212	Wilson, Jan	416715
James, Linda	624621	Wyatt, Mark	321326
Lane, Arthur	115702		

10. According to the list, the number of women referred to the laboratory during January was
    A. 4   B. 5   C. 6   D. 7

11. The clinic from which the MOST patients were referred was
    A. Cardiac
    B. Gynecology
    C. Ophthalmology
    D. Pediatrics

12. The YOUNGEST patient referred from any clinic other than Pediatrics was
    A. Leslie Black
    B. Marie Cook
    C. Arthur Lane
    D. Sally Saunders

13. The number of patients whose laboratory tests were performed on or before January 16 was
    A. 7   B. 8   C. 9   D. 10

14. The number of patients referred for laboratory tests who are under age 45 is
    A. 7   B. 8   C. 9   D. 10

15. The OLDEST patient referred to the clinic during January was
    A. Jacqueline Adams
    B. Linda James
    C. Arthur Lane
    D. Jan Wilson

16. The ONLY patient treated in the Orthopedics clinic was
    A. Marie Cook
    B. Pat Fisher
    C. Ellen Rogers
    D. Jan Wilson

17. A woman, age 37 was referred from the Hematology clinic to the laboratory. Her laboratory tests were performed on January 9. Her identification number would be
    A. 610937   B. 623709   C. 613790   D. 623790

18. A man was referred for lab tests from the Orthopedics clinic. He is 30 years old and his tests were performed on January 6.
    His identification number would be
    A. 413006   B. 510360   C. 513006   D. 513060

    18.____

19. A 4-year-old boy was referred from the Pediatrics clinic to have laboratory tests on January 23.
    His identification number was
    A. 310422   B. 310423   C. 310433   D. 320403

    19.____

KEY (CORRECT ANSWERS)

1.	B	11.	D
2.	B	12.	B
3.	B	13.	A
4.	D	14.	C
5.	D	15.	D
6.	B	16.	A
7.	A	17.	B
8.	D	18.	C
9.	C	19.	B
10.	B		

TEST 4

DIRECTIONS: Each question or incomplete statement is followed by several suggested answers or completions. Select the one that BEST answers the question or completes the statement. *PRINT THE LETTER OF THE CORRECT ANSWER IN THE SPACE AT THE RIGHT.*

Questions 1-10.

DIRECTIONS: Questions 1 through 10 are to be answered on the basis of the information and directions given below.

Assume that you are a Senior Stenographer assigned to the personnel bureau of a city agency. Your supervisor has asked you to classify the employees in your agency into the following five groups:

- A. Employees who are college graduates, who are at least 35 years of age but less than 50, and who have been employed by the City for five years or more;
- B. Employees who have been employed by the City for less than five years, who are not college graduates, and who earn at least $32,500 a year but less than $34,500;
- C. Employees who have been City employees for five years or more, who are at least 21 years of age but less than 35, and who are not college graduates;
- D. Employee who earn at least $34,500 a year but less than $36,000 who are college graduates, and who have been employed by the City for less than five years;
- E. Employees who are not included in any of the foregoing groups.

NOTE: In classifying these employees you are to compute age and period of service as of January 1, 2003. In all cases, it is to be assumed that each employee has been employed continuously in City service. In each question, consider only the information which will assist you in classifying each employee Any information which is of no assistance in classifying an employee would not be considered.

SAMPLE: Mr. Brown, a 29-year-old veteran, was appointed to his present position of Clerk on June 1, 2000. He has completed two years of college. His present salary is $33,050.

The correct answer to this sample is B, since the employee has been employed by the City for less than five years, is not a college graduate, and earn at least $32,500 a year but less than $34,500.

Questions 1 through 10 contain excerpts from the personnel records of 10 employees in the agency. In the correspondingly numbered space at the right print the capital letter preceding the appropriate group into which you would place each employee.

1. Mr. James has been employed by the City since 1993, when he was graduated from a local college. Now 35 years of age, he earns $36,000 a year.   1.____

2. Mr. Worth began working in City service early in 1999. He was awarded his college degree in 1994, at the age of 21. As a result of a recent promotion, he now earns $34,500 a year.   2.____

3. Miss Thomas has been a City employee since August 1, 1998. Her salary is $34,500 a year. Miss Thomas, who is 25 years old, has had only three years of high school training.

3.____

4. Mr. Williams has had three promotions since entering City service on January 1, 1991. He was graduated from college with honors in 1974, when he was 20 years of age. His present salary is $37,000 a year.

4.____

5. Miss Jones left college after two years of study to take an appointment to a position in the City service paying $33,300 a year. She began work on March 1, 1997 when she was 19 years of age.

5.____

6. Mr. Smith was graduated from an engineering college with honors in January 1998 and became a City employee three months later. His present salary is $35,810. Mr. Smith was born in 1976.

6.____

7. Miss Earnest was born on May 31, 1979. Her education consisted of four years of high school and one year of business school. She was appointed as a typist in a City agency on June 1, 1997. Her annual salary is $33,500.

7.____

8. Mr. Adams, a 24-year-old clerk, began his City service on July 1, 1999, soon after being discharged from the U.S. Army. A college graduate, his present annual salary is $33,200.

8.____

9. Miss Charles attends college in the evenings, hoping to obtain her degree is 2004, when she will be 30 years of age. She has been a City employee since April 1998, and earns $33,350.

9.____

10. Mr. Dolan was just promoted to his present position after six years of City service. He was graduated from high school in 1982, when he was 18 years of age, but did not go on to college. Mr. Dolan's present salary is $33,500.

10.____

KEY (CORRECT ANSWERS)

1.	A	6.	D
2.	D	7.	C
3.	E	8.	E
4.	A	9.	B
5.	C	10.	E

TEST 5

DIRECTIONS: Questions 1 through 4 each contain five numbers that should be arranged in numerical order. The number with the lowest numerical value should be first and the number with the highest numerical value should be last. Pick that option which indicates the CORRECT order of the numbers.

       Examples: A. 9; 18; 14; 15; 27
                           B. 9; 14; 15; 18; 27
                           C. 14; 15; 18; 27; 9
                           D. 9; 14; 15; 27; 18

The correct answer is B, which contains the proper arrangement of the five numbers.

1.   A.   20573; 20753; 20738; 20837; 20098
      B.   20098; 20753; 20573; 20738; 20837
      C.   20098; 20573; 20753; 20837; 20738
      D.   20098; 20573; 20738; 20753; 20837

2.   A.   113492; 113429; 111314; 113114; 131413
      B.   111314; 113114; 113429; 113492; 131413
      C.   111314; 113429; 113492; 113114; 131413
      D.   111314; 113114; 131413; 113429; 113492

3.   A.   1029763; 1030421; 1035681; 1036928; 1067391
      B.   1030421; 1029763; 1035681; 1067391; 1036928
      C.   1030421; 1035681; 1036928; 1067391; 1029763
      D.   1029763; 1039421; 1035681; 1067391; 1036928

4.   A.   1112315; 1112326; 1112337; 1112349; 1112306
      B.   1112306; 1112315; 1112337; 1112326; 1112349
      C.   1112306; 1112315; 1112326; 1112337; 1112349
      D.   1112306; 1112326; 1112315; 1112337; 1112349

KEY (CORRECT ANSWERS)

1. D
2. B
3. A
4. C

TEST 6

DIRECTIONS: The phonetic filing system is a method of filing names in which the alphabet is reduced to key code letters. The six key letters and their equivalents are as follows:

KEY LETTERS	EQUIVALENTS
b	p, f, v
c	s, k, g, j, q, x, z
d	t
l	none
m	n
r	none

A key letter represents itself.
Vowels (a, e, i, o, and u) and the letters w, h, and y are omitted.
For example, the name GILMAN would be represented as follows:
    G is represented by the key letter C.
    I is a vowel and is omitted.
    L is a letter and represents itself.
    M is a key letter and represents itself.
    A is a vowel and is omitted.
    N is represented by the key letter M.

Therefore, the phonetic filing code for the name GILMAN is CLMM.

Answer Questions 1 through 10 based on the information below.

1. The phonetic filing code for the name FITZGERALD would be
   A. BDCCRLD   B. BDCRLD   C. BDZCRLD   D. BTZCRLD

2. The phonetic filing code CLBR may represent any one of the following names EXCEPT
   A. Calprey   B. Flower   C. Glover   D. Silver

3. The phonetic filing code LDM may represent any one of the following names EXCEPT
   A. Halden   B. Hilton   C. Walton   D. Wilson

4. The phonetic filing code for the name RODRIGUEZ would be
   A. RDRC   B. RDRCC   C. RDRCZ   D. RTRCC

5. The phonetic filing code for the name MAXWELL would be
   A. MCLL   B. MCWL   C. MCWLL   D. MXLL

6. The phonetic filing code for the name ANDERSON would be
   A. AMDRCM   B. ENDRSM   C. MDRCM   D. NDERCN

7. The phonetic filing code for the name SAVITSKY would be
   A. CBDCC   B. CBDCY   C. SBDCC   D. SVDCC

1.____
2.____
3.____
4.____
5.____
6.____
7.____

2 (#6)

8. The phonetic filing code CMC may represent any one of the following names EXCEPT 8._____
   A. James   B. Jayes   C. Johns   D. Jones

9. The ONLY one of the following names that could be represented by the phonetic filing code CDDDM would be 9._____
   A. Catalano   B. Chesterton   C. Cittadino   D. Cuttlerman

10. The ONLY one of the following names that could be represented by the phonetic filing code LLMCM would be 10._____
    A. Ellington   B. Hallerman   C. Inslerman   D. Willingham

KEY (CORRECT ANSWERS)

1. A   6. C
2. B   7. A
3. D   8. B
4. B   9. C
5. A   10. D

INTERPRETING STATISTICAL DATA GRAPHS, CHARTS AND TABLES
EXAMINATION SECTION
TEST 1

DIRECTIONS: Each question or incomplete statement is followed by several suggested answers or completions. Select the one that BEST answers the question or completes the statement. *PRINT THE LETTER OF THE CORRECT ANSWER IN THE SPACE AT THE RIGHT.*

Questions 1-4.

DIRECTIONS: Questions 1 through 4 are to be answered SOLELY on the basis of the following table.

STOLEN AND RECOVERED PROPERTY IN COMMUNITY X 2018-2019				
Type of Property	Value of Property Stolen		Value of Property Recovered	
	2018	2019	2018	2019
Currency	$264,925	$204,534	$10,579	$13,527
Jewelry	165,317	106,885	20,913	20,756
Furs	10,007	24,028	105	1,620
Clothing	62,265	49,219	4,322 7	15,821
Automobiles	740,719	606,062	36,701	558,442
Miscellaneous	356,901	351,064	62,077	103,117
TOTAL	$1,600,134	$1,341,792	$834,697	$713,283

1. Of the following types of property, the one which shows the HIGHEST ratio of *value of property recovered* to *value of property stolen* is   1.____

   A. clothing for 2018   B. currency for 2018
   C. jewelry for 2019   D. miscellaneous for 2019

2. Of the types of property which show a decrease from 2018 to 2019 in the value of property stolen, the one which shows the GREATEST percentage decrease in the value of the property recovered is   2.____

   A. automobiles   B. currency
   C. furs   D. jewelry

3. According to the above table, the total value of currency and jewelry stolen in 2019, as compared to 2018, decreased APPROXIMATELY by   3.____

   A. 3%   B. 20%   C. 28%   D. 38%

111

4. According to the above table, the TOTAL value of all types of property recovered was
   A. a slightly lower percentage of the value of property stolen for 2018 than for 2019
   B. less for the year 2018 than the value of any individual type of property recovered for the year 2019
   C. approximately 60% of the value of all property stolen in 2018 and approximately 70% in 2019
   D. greater for the year 2019 than the value of any individual type of property recovered for the year 2018

4._____

KEY (CORRECT ANSWERS)

1. D
2. A
3. C
4. A

TEST 2

Questions 1-6.

DIRECTIONS: Questions 1 through 6 are to be answered SOLELY on the basis of the information supplied in the chart below.

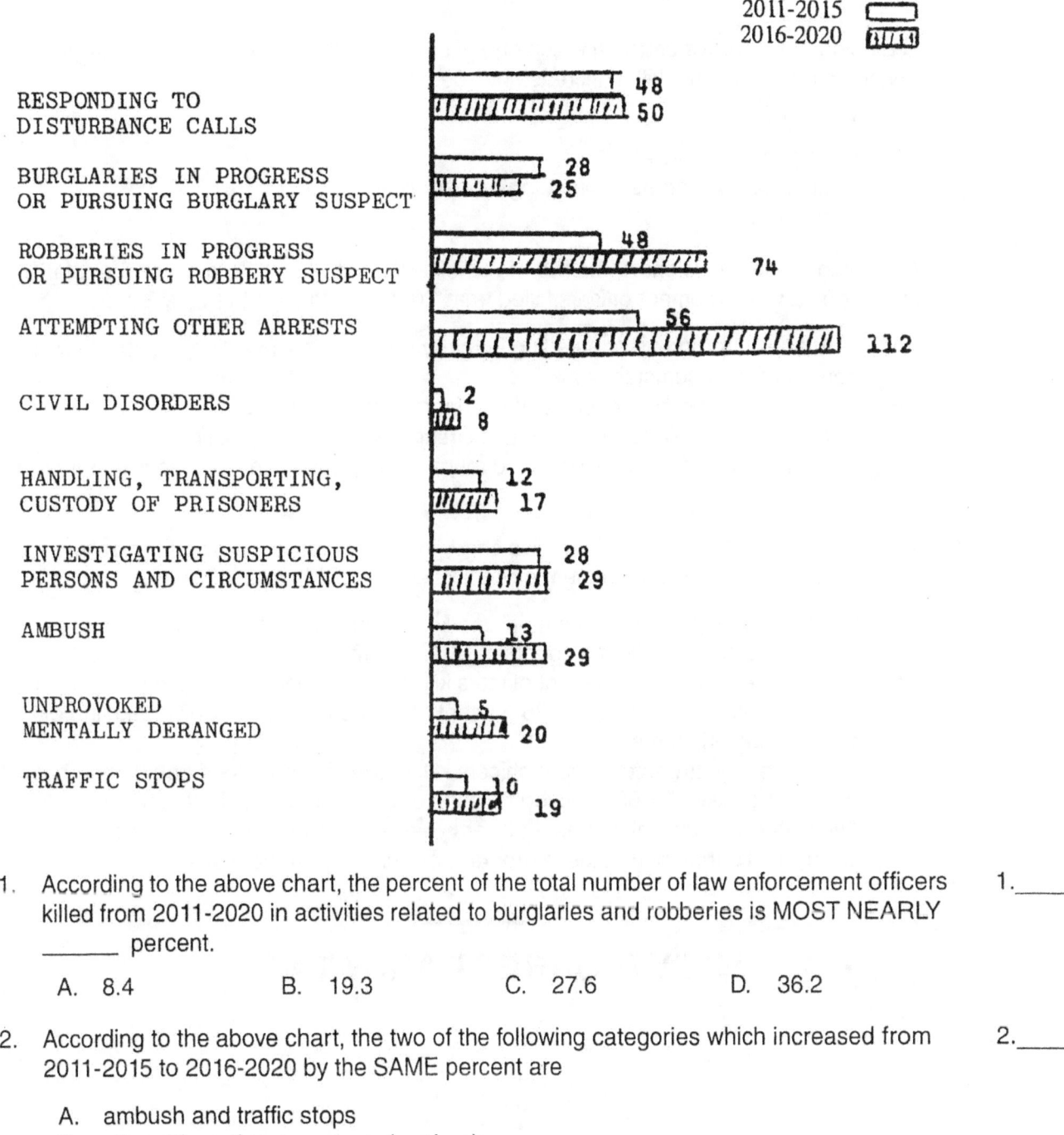

1. According to the above chart, the percent of the total number of law enforcement officers killed from 2011-2020 in activities related to burglaries and robberies is MOST NEARLY _____ percent.

   A. 8.4   B. 19.3   C. 27.6   D. 36.2

2. According to the above chart, the two of the following categories which increased from 2011-2015 to 2016-2020 by the SAME percent are

   A. ambush and traffic stops
   B. attempting other arrests and ambush

2 (#2)

C. civil disorders and unprovoked mentally deranged
D. response to disturbance calls and investigating suspicious persons and circumstances

3. According to the above chart, the percentage increase in law enforcement officers killed from the 2011-2015 period to the 2016-2020 period is MOST NEARLY _____ percent.

A. 34   B. 53   C. 65   D. 100

4. According to the above chart, in which one of the following activities did the number of law enforcement officers killed increase by 100 percent?

A. Ambush
B. Attempting other arrests
C. Robberies in progress or pursuing robbery suspect
D. Traffic stops

5. According to the above chart, the two of the following activities during which the total number of law enforcement officers killed from 2011 to 2020 was the SAME are

A. burglaries in progress or pursuing burglary suspect and investigating suspicious persons and circumstances
B. handling, transporting, custody of prisoners and traffic stops
C. investigating suspicious persons and circumstances and ambush
D. responding to disturbance calls and robberies in progress or pursuing robbery suspect

6. According to the categories in the above chart, the one of the following statements which can be made about law enforcement officers killed from 2011 to 2015 is that

A. the number of law enforcement officers killed during civil disorders equals one-sixth of the number killed responding to disturbance calls
B. the number of law enforcement officers killed during robberies in progress or pursuing robbery suspect equals 25 percent of the number killed while handling or transporting prisoners
C. the number of law enforcement officers killed during traffic stops equals one-half the number killed for unprovoked reasons or by the mentally deranged
D. twice as many law enforcement officers were killed attempting other arrests as were killed during burglaries in progress or pursuing burglary suspect

KEY (CORRECT ANSWERS)

1. C
2. C
3. B
4. B
5. B
6. D

TEST 3

Questions 1-6.

DIRECTIONS: Questions 1 through 6 are to be answered SOLELY on the basis of the graph below.

YEARLY INCIDENCE OF MAJOR CRIMES FOR COMMUNITY Z
2017-2019

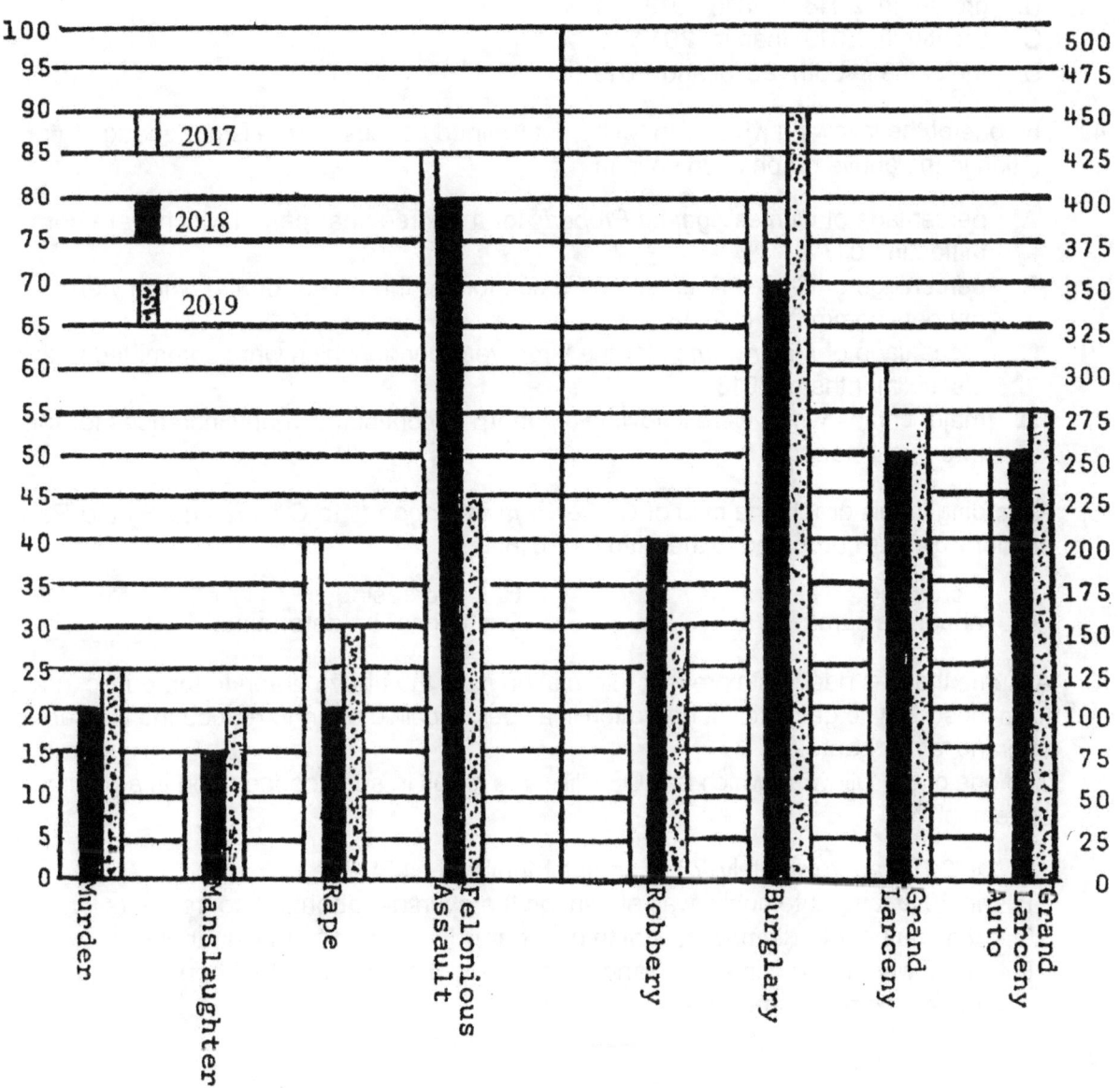

CRIMES AGAINST THE PERSON   CRIMES AGAINST PROPERTY

115

1. Of the following crimes, the one for which the 2019 figure was GREATER than the average of the previous two years was

   A. grand larceny
   B. manslaughter
   C. rape
   D. robbery

2. If the incidence of burglary in 2020 were to increase over 2019 by the same number as it increased in 2019 over 2018, then the average for this crime for the four-year period from 2017 through 2020 would be MOST NEARLY

   A. 100　　B. 400　　C. 415　　D. 440

3. The above graph indicates that the percentage INCREASE in grand larceny auto over the previous year was

   A. greater in 2019 than in 2018
   B. greater in 2018 than in 2019
   C. greater in 2019 than in 2017
   D. the same in both 2018 and 2019

4. The one of the following which cannot be determined because there is not enough information in the above graph to do so is the

   A. percentage of Crimes Against Property for the three-year period which were committed in 2017
   B. percentage of Crimes Against the Person for the three-year period which were murders committed in 2018
   C. percentage of Major Crimes for the three-year period which were committed in the first six months of 2018
   D. major crimes which were following a pattern of continuing yearly increases for the three-year period

5. According to this graph, the ratio of Crimes Against Property to Crimes Against the Person for 2019, as compared to the ratio for 2018, is

   A. increasing
   B. decreasing
   C. about the same
   D. cannot be determined

6. Assume that it is desired to present information from the above graph to the public in a form most likely to gain their cooperation in a special police effort to reduce the incidence of grand larceny auto.
   The one of the following which is MOST likely to result in such cooperation is a public statement that

   A. in 2019, approximately .75 of an automobile was stolen every day
   B. in 2019, one automobile was stolen, on the average, about 32 hours hours
   C. the number of automobiles stolen per year will increase from year to year
   D. there were more crimes of grand larceny auto than crimes of robbery committed during the past three years

KEY (CORRECT ANSWERS)

1. B　　4. C
2. D　　5. A
3. B　　6. B

TEST 4

Questions 1-7.

DIRECTIONS: Questions 1 through 7 are to be answered SOLELY on the basis of the information contained in the following tables and chart.

TABLE 1

Number of Murders by Region, United States: 2014 and 2015

Region	Year	
	2014	2015
Northeastern States	2,521	2,849
North Central States	3,427	3,697
Southern States	6,577	7,055
Western States	2,062	2,211

Number in each case for given year and region represents total number (100%) of murders in that region for that year.

TABLE 2

Murder by Circumstance, U.S. - 2015
(Percent distribution by category)

Region	Total	Spouse Killing spouse	Parent Killing child	Other family killings	Romantic triangle and lovers' quarrels	Other arguments	Known Felony type	Suspected felony type
Northeastern States	100.0	9.6	3.7	6.1	7.9	38.4	25.4	8.9
North Central States	100.0	11.3	3.0	8.9	5.0	39.5	22.4	9.9
Southern States	100.0	13.8	2.2	8.8	8.4	46.0	13.9	6.9
Western States	100.0	12.5	4.9	7.0	6.4	32.2	28.0	9.0

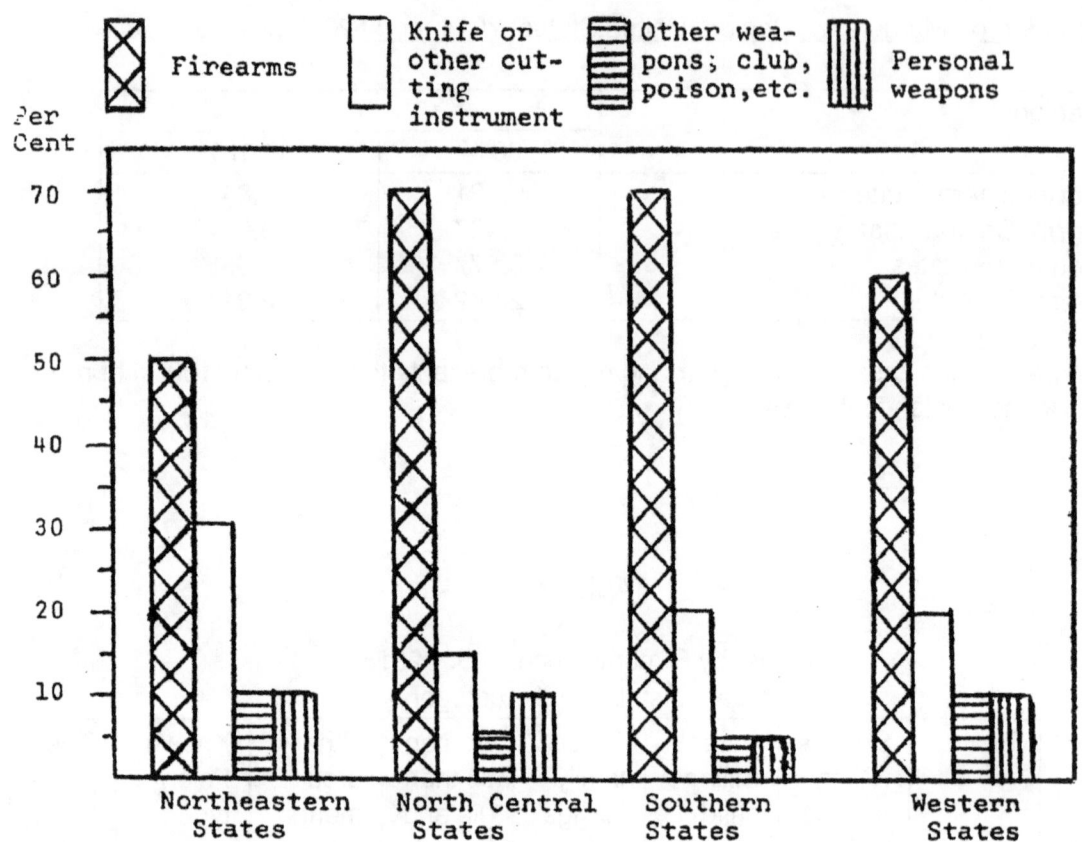

CHART 1
Murder by Type of Weapon Used, U.S. - 2015
(Percent Distribution)

1. The number of persons murdered by firearms in the Western States in 2015 was MOST NEARLY

    A. 220 B. 445 C. 1235 D. 1325

2. In 2015, the number of murders in the category *Parent killing child* was GREATEST in the _____ States.

    A. Northeastern B. North Central
    C. Southern D. Western

3. The difference between the number of persons murdered with firearms and the number of persons murdered with other weapons (club, poison, etc.) in the North Central States in 2015 is MOST NEARLY

    A. 2200 B. 2400 C. 2600 D. 2800

4. In 2014, the ratio of the number of murders in the Western States to the total number of murders in the U.S. was MOST NEARLY

    A. 1 to 4 B. 1 to 5 C. 1 to 7 D. 1 to 9

5. The total number of murders in the U.S. in the category of *Romantic triangles and lovers'* 5.____
   quarrels in 2015 was MOST NEARLY

   A. 850 B. 950 C. 1050 D. 1150

6. Which of the following represents the GREATEST number of murders in 2015? 6.____
   Persons murdered by

   A. firearms in the Western States
   B. knives or other cutting instruments in the Southern States
   C. knives or other cutting instruments and persons murdered by other weapons (club, poison, etc.) in the Northeastern States
   D. knives or other cutting instruments, persons murdered by other weapons (club, poison, etc.) and persons murdered by personal weapons in the North Central States

7. From 2014 to 2015, the total number of murders increased by the GREATEST percentage in the _____ States. 7.____

   A. Northeastern B. North Central
   C. Southern D. Western

KEY (CORRECT ANSWERS)

1. D
2. C
3. B
4. C
5. D
6. B
7. A

TEST 5

Questions 1-5.

DIRECTIONS: Questions 1 through 5 are to be answered SOLELY on the basis of the following.

DISTRIBUTION OF CITIZENS' RESPONSES TO STATEMENTS CONCERNING SHERIFFS' ARRESTS
(Number of citizens responding = 1171)

	CATEGORIES				
	(A) Strongly Agree	(B) Agree	(C) Disagree	(D) Strongly Disagree	(E) Don't Know
I. Sheriffs act improperly in arresting defendants, even when these persons are rude and ill-mannered	12%	37%	36%	9%	6%
II. Sheriffs frequently use more force than necessary when making arrests	9%	19%	46%	19%	7%
III. Any defendant who insults or physically abuses a sheriff has no complaint if he is sternly handled in return	13%	44%	32%	7%	4%

1. The total percentage of responses to Statement III OTHER THAN *Strongly Agree* and *Disagree* is

    A. 45%   B. 46%   C. 55%   D. 59%

2. The number of *Disagree* responses to Statement II is MOST NEARLY

    A. 71   B. 114   C. 539   D. 820

3. Assume that for Statement II the (B) percentage of responses were doubled and the (A) percentage increased one and a half times.
If the (D) and (E) percentages remained the same, the (C) percentage would then MOST NEARLY be

   A. 23%   B. 26%   C. 39%   D. 52%

   3.____

4. The total number of *Don't Know* responses is MOST NEARLY

   A. 17
   B. 188
   C. 200
   D. a figure which cannot be determined from the table

   4.____

5. If the percentage of Disagree responses to Statement III were 35% less, the resulting percentage would MOST NEARLY be

   A. 11%   B. 14%   C. 15%   D. 21%

   5.____

KEY (CORRECT ANSWERS)

1. C
2. C
3. A
4. C
5. D

TEST 6

Questions 1-3.

DIRECTIONS: Questions 1 through 3 are to be answered SOLELY on the basis of the statistical report given below.

The following is a statistical report of the activities of the bureau during the current year as compared with the previous year.

	Current Year	Previous Year
Memoranda of law prepared	68	83
Legal matters forwarded to Corporation Counsel	122	144
Letters requesting legal information	756	807
Letters requesting departmental records	139	111
Matters for publication	17	26
Court appearances of members of bureau	4,678	4,621
Conferences	94	103
Lectures at Police Academy	30	33
Reports on proposed legislation	194	255
Deciphering of codes	79	27
Expert testimony	31	16
Notices to court witnesses	55	81
Briefs prepared	22	18
Court papers prepared	258	

1. According to the report, the percentage of bills prepared and sponsored by the Legal Bureau which were passed by the State Legislature and sent to the Governor for approval was APPROXIMATELY

    A. 3.1%
    B. 2.6%
    C. .5%
    D. not capable of determination from the data given

2. According to the statistical report, the activity showing the GREATEST percentage of decrease in the current year as compared with the previous year was

    A. matters for publication
    B. reports on proposed legislation

1.____

2.____

122

C. notices to court witnesses
D. memoranda of law prepared

3. According to the statistical report, the activity showing the GREATEST percentage of *increase* in the current year as compared with the previous year was

   A. court appearances of members of the bureau
   B. giving expert testimony
   C. deciphering of codes
   D. letters requesting departmental records

KEY (CORRECT ANSWERS)

1. D
2. A
3. C

TEST 7

Questions 1-5.

DIRECTIONS: Questions 1 through 5 are to be answered SOLELY on the basis of the information contained in Tables I and II that appear below and on the following page.

TABLE I
NUMBER OF ARRESTS FOR VARIOUS CRIMES AND DISPOSITION

OFFENSES	TOTAL ARRESTED	INVESTIGATED AND RELEASED	HELD FOR PROSECUTION	GUILTY AS CHARGED	GUILTY OF LESSER OFFENSES	DISPOSITION OTHER THAN CONVICTION
Murder	48	10	38	12	9	17
Rape	41	10	31	8	3	20
Aggravated assault	241	106	135	36	32	67
Robbery	351	177	174	98	35	41
Burglary	890	371	519	322	88	109
Larceny	1,665	466 78	1,199	929	58	212
Auto theft	464		386	278	46	62
TOTAL	3,700	1,218	2,482	1,683	271	528

TABLE II

ARRESTS FOR LARCENY - PERCENTAGE OF SUCH ARRESTS BY AGE AND SEX

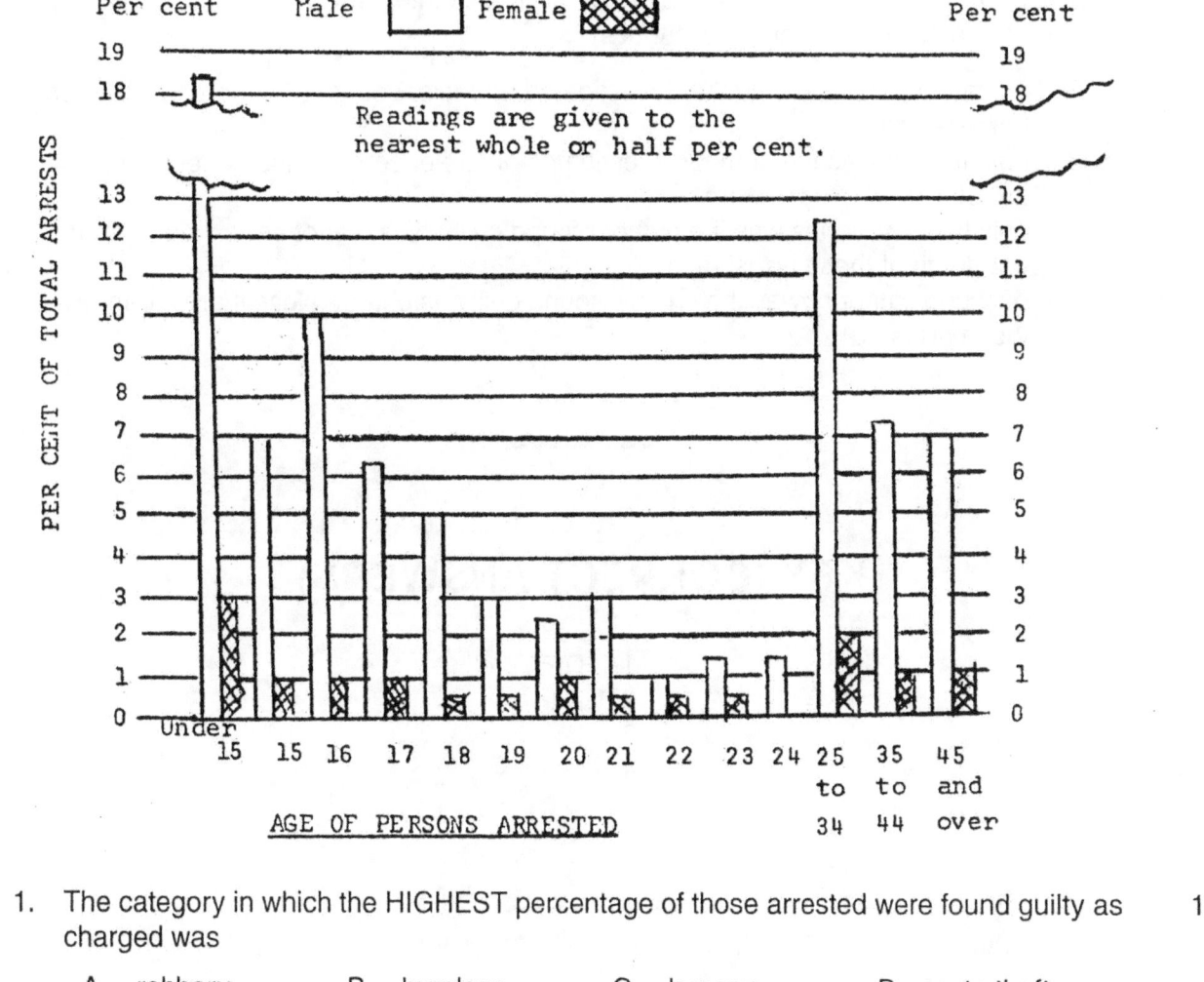

1. The category in which the HIGHEST percentage of those arrested were found guilty as charged was

    A. robbery
    B. burglary
    C. larceny
    D. auto theft

2. The number of 21-year-olds, both males and females, arrested for larceny is MOST NEARLY

    A. 29
    B. 37
    C. 42
    D. 58

3. The total number of males arrested for larceny, as compared to the number of females arrested for larceny, is _____ times as great.

    A. 5
    B. 6
    C. 8
    D. 10

4. Considering only the category of larceny, the one of the following statements which is INCORRECT is:

    A. The percentage of 25-year-old males arrested cannot be determined
    B. Twice as many 16-year-old males were arrested as 18-year-old males

C. The percentage of 16-year-old males arrested was twice as high as the percentage of 18-year-old males
D. Persons 19 years of age and younger accounted for exactly half of the total arrests for larceny

5. The one of the following which is the MOST accurate statement with respect to the disposition of arrests in each category is that in

   A. no category was the number investigated and released greater than half the number arrested
   B. no category was the number investigated and released less than one-fifth of those arrested
   C. only two categories was the number found guilty of lesser offense greater than one-tenth of those arrested
   D. only one category was the number found guilty as charged less than one-fourth of those arrested

5.____

KEY (CORRECT ANSWERS)

1. D
2. D
3. B
4. D
5. C

TEST 8

Questions 1-5.

DIRECTIONS: Questions 1 through 5 are to be answered SOLELY on the basis of the table below.

VALUE OF PROPERTY STOLEN - 2017 AND 2018
LARCENY

Category	2017		2018	
	Number of Offenses	Value of Stolen Property	Number of Offense	Value of Stolen Property
Pocket-picking	20	$1,950	10	$ 950
Purse-snatching	175	5,750	20	12,500
Shoplifting	155	7,950	225	17,350
Automobile thefts	1,040	127,050	860	108,000
Thefts of auto accessories	1,135	34,950	970	24,400
Bicycle thefts	355	8,250	240	6,350
All other thefts	1,375	187,150	1,300	153,150

1. Of the total number of larcenies reported for 2017, automobile thefts accounted for MOST NEARLY

   A. 5%   B. 15%   C. 25%   D. 50%

2. The LARGEST percentage decrease in the value of the stolen property from 2017 to 2018 was in the category of

   A. pocket-picking
   B. automobile thefts
   C. thefts of automobile accessories
   D. bicycle thefts

3. In 2018, the average amount of each theft was LOWEST for the category of

   A. pocket-picking
   B. purse-snatching
   C. shoplifting
   D. thefts of auto accessories

4. The category which had the LARGEST numerical reduction in the number of offenses from 2017 to 2018 was

   A. pocket-picking
   B. automobile thefts
   C. thefts of auto accessories
   D. bicycle thefts

5. When the categories are ranked for each year according to the number of offenses committed in each category (largest number to rank first), the number of categories which will have the SAME rank in 2017 as in 2018 is

   A. 3   B. 4   C. 5   D. 6

5._____

KEY (CORRECT ANSWERS)

1. C
2. A
3. D
4. B
5. C

TEST 9

Questions 1-5.

DIRECTIONS: Questions 1 through 5 are to be answered SOLELY on the basis of the graphs below.

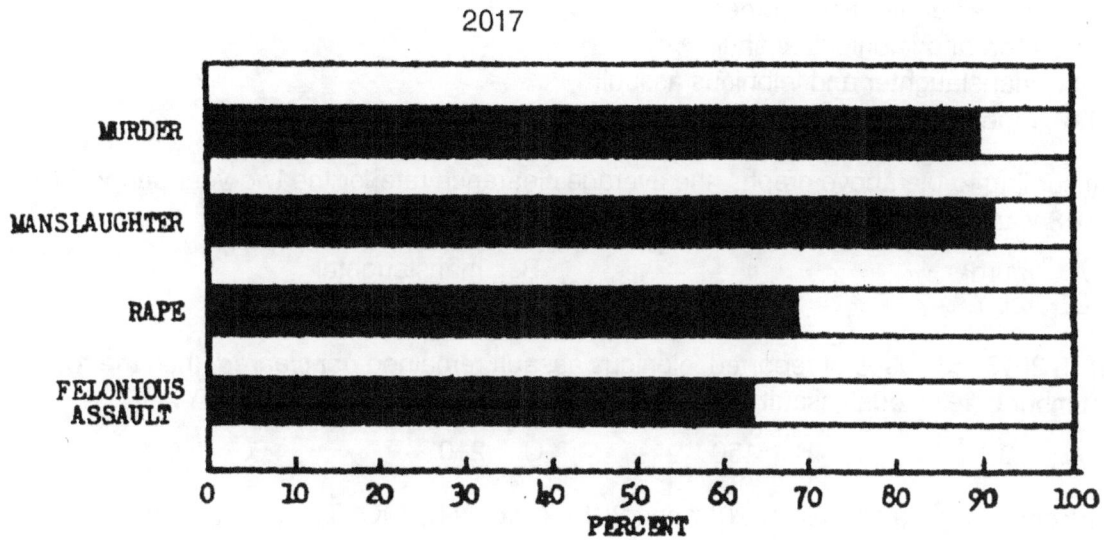

2017

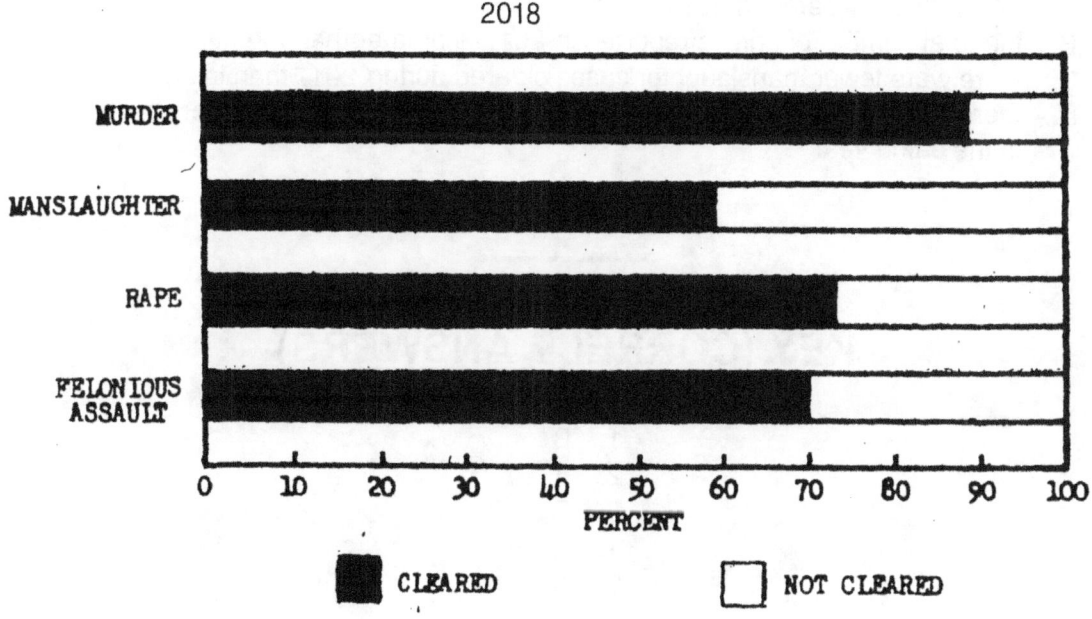

2018

CLEARED   NOT CLEARED

NOTE: The clearance rate is defined as the percentage of reported cases which were closed by the police through arrests or other means.

1. According to the above graphs, the AVERAGE clearance rate for all four crimes for 2018   1._____
   A. was greater than in 2017
   B. was less than in 2017

C. was the same as in 2017
D. cannot properly be compared to the 2017 figures

2. According to the above graphs, the crimes which did NOT show an increasing clearance rate from 2017 to 2018 were

   A. manslaughter and murder
   B. rape and felonious assault
   C. manslaughter and felonious assault
   D. rape and murder

3. According to the above graphs, the average clearance rate for the two-year period 2017-2018 was SMALLEST for the crime of

   A. murder
   B. manslaughter
   C. rape
   D. felonious assault

4. If, in 2018, 63 cases of reported felonious assault remained *not cleared,* then the total number of felonious assault cases reported that year was MOST NEARLY

   A. 90
   B. 150
   C. 210
   D. 900

5. In comparing the graphs for 2017 and 2018, it would be MOST accurate to state that

   A. it is not possible to compare the total number of crimes cleared in 2017 with the total number cleared in 2018
   B. the total number of crimes reported in 2017 is greater than the number in 2018
   C. there were fewer manslaughter cases cleared during 2017 than in 2018
   D. there were more rape cases cleared during 2018 than manslaughter cases cleared in the same year

KEY (CORRECT ANSWERS)

1. B
2. A
3. D
4. C
5. A

TEST 10

Questions 1-5.

DIRECTIONS: Questions 1 through 5 are to be answered SOLELY on the basis of the following chart.

FATAL HIGHWAY ACCIDENTS

	Drivers Over 18 Years of Age			Drivers 18 Years of Age And Under		
2018	Auto	Other Vehicles	Total	Auto	Other Vehicles	Total
January	43	0	43	4	0	4
February	52	0	52	10	0	10
March	36	0	36	8	0	8
April	50	0	50	17	0	17
May	40	2	42	5	0	5
June	26	0	26	8	0	8
July	29	0	29	6	0	6
August	29	1	30	3	0	3
September	36	0	36	4	0	4
October	45	1	46	2	1	3
November	54	1	55	3	0	3
December	66	1	67	3	0	6
TOTALS	506	6	512	76	1	77

1. The average number of fatal auto accidents per month during 2018 involving drivers older than eighteen was MOST NEARLY

    A. 42 B. 43 C. 44 D. 45

2. The TOTAL number of fatal highway accidents during 2018 was

    A. 506 B. 512 C. 582 D. 589

3. The month during which the LOWEST number of fatal highway accidents occurred was

    A. March B. June C. July D. August

1.___

2.___

3.___

2 (#10)

4. Of the total number of fatal highway accidents during 2018 involving drivers older than eighteen, the percentage of accidents which took place during December is MOST NEARLY

   A. 10 B. 13 C. 16 D. 19

5. The GREATEST percentage drop in fatal highway accidents occurred from

   A. February to March B. April to May
   C. June to July D. July to Augus

KEY (CORRECT ANSWERS)

1. A
2. D
3. D
4. B
5. B

POLICE SCIENCE NOTES

COLLECTION, IDENTIFICATION AND PRESERVATION OF EVIDENCE

The Definition and importance of Evidence

Definition

Evidence can be defined as "any medium of proof or probative matter, legally presented at the trial of any issue, by the participants of the trial and through the medium of witnesses, records, documents, objects, etc., for the purpose of inducing belief in the minds of the court and the jurors as to its creditability and contention." In more general terms, evidence is anything that can be legally presented to indicate the guilt of a criminal act or to aid in determining the truth about any fact in question.

Importance

The primary importance of evidence is the aid it offers in the identification of the guilty party and in his successful prosecution. Because of this, the proper collection, identification, and preservation of evidence make up a vital part of police operations. Cases may be won or lost depending upon the proficiency of the police department in this area.

Evidence is the means by which the patrolman or investigator can aid the prosecutor in giving the court a complete picture of the crime and its commission. It explains the facts that the officer uses to determine that the accused is guilty. Properly prepared and presented, evidence may serve the same purpose as taking the court and the jury to the scene of the crime and reconstructing the events which led to the commission of the crime charged.

In order to insure that this vital function is performed properly, most departments have specialists known as criminal investigators to collect, search and properly evaluate evidence. The reason for this is that such specialization saves time and leaves the patrolman free to resume his primary duties once the investigator arrives at the scene. However, since the general patrolman or the auxiliary policeman will usually be the first to arrive at the scene and therefore is crucial to the outcome of the criminal investigation, it is important that they have an adequate understanding of evidence and be skilled in its preservation and protection. The need for developing adequate investigative skills is especially crucial in those departments without a specialist and where the officers are expected to conduct their own investigation.

Classification of Evidence

Evidence may be divided into three major classifications:

DIRECT evidence directly establishes the main fact of issue. It applies immediately to the fact to be proven or disproven and is usually what a person sees, hears, or knows.

CIRCUMSTANTIAL evidence tends to prove or disprove the fact in issue by other facts leading to a presumption of the truth or falsity of the main fact. The essence here is inference-establishing a factor or circumstance from which a court may infer another fact. It may be real evidence or things which may be said to "speak for themselves." Ownership of the murder weapon, the fingerprints thereon, and the inability of the accused to account for his actions at the time of the crime would be matters of circumstantial evidence.

REAL OR PHYSICAL evidence comprises those tangible objects introduced at the trial which speak for themselves and need no explanation, just identification. Examples of real evidence would be guns, fingerprints, and bloodstains. Real evidence can be further divided into:

FIXED OR IMMOVABLE evidence which by its very nature cannot be moved from the crime scene. It includes such objects as latent fingerprints, tool marks, doors, windows, wall plaster, etc. Of course, fingerprints may be lifted, casts made of foot and tire marks, and photographs taken of the entire scene; but the actual object remains incapable of being transported to the courtroom.

MOVABLE evidence which can be preserved intact for examination at headquarters and presentation in the courtroom. This includes such objects as bullets, tools, hair, documents, clothing, and many other similar objects.

Chain of Custody - The Cardinal Rule of Evidence

In order for the evidence to be properly admitted into court, its location and holder must be accurately established from the time the officer or investigator finds the evidence until it is presented in court. If the whereabouts of the evidence cannot be established, even for a moment, the court will rule it is inadmissible. The reason for this is because if it can be shown that the evidence was out of responsible hands or unaccountable for, then it is also likely that the evidence could have been tampered with thereby negating its validity and leaving the court no alternative but to dismiss it. Therefore, in order to overcome the questions presented by the defense and to impress the judge and jury that the evidence has been properly protected, the police officer must establish an accurate "chain of custody" for each piece of evidence presented in court.

Perhaps the best method of maintaining an accurate chain of custody is through the use of receipts. If the evidence is to be out of the officer's hand for even a minute he should demand a receipt containing: the time, date, and place where the exchange occurred, to whom the evidence was given, and for what purpose. Likewise, if the officer receives any evidence for transportation or for other purposes he should fill out and give a receipt to the person giving him the evidence.

Collection of Evidence

Two points to be remembered by all personnel concerned with the collection of evidence are: (1) there, is rarely a major crime committed without some kind of evidence being left at the scene, and (2) nothing at a crime scene is too significant to be overlooked. The ultimate success of any investigation will depend on the acumen of the officers in searching the scene, recognizing evidence, and preserving it.

Preliminary Activities at the Crime Scene

The first officer at the crime scene who will usually be either the beat patrolman or the auxiliary policeman should:
1. Assist the injured when necessary.
2. Notify the proper experts and equipment to conduct a proper crime scene examination.
3. Obtain pertinent data from the witnesses and any suspects, keeping them separated if possible.
4. Use the most effective means possible to protect the crime scene from any intrusions by unauthorized personnel.
5. Arrest any perpetrators caught at or near the scene.
6. Assist the investigator when he arrives to examine the scene.

The investigator or whoever is in charge of the investigation should determine from the initial officer what has been done and what needs to be done before taking command of the situation. He will then conduct a thorough investigation of the scene and question all witnesses, victims, and suspects at the scene.

Examination of the Crime Scene

Usually the first person to be admitted to the crime scene is the photographer who will take as many photographs as necessary to insure proper coverage of the scene for further study and analysis. While the photographer is shooting the scene, the investigator will make a sketch of the scene to supplement the photographs by adding the dimensions of height, distances, and locations of the scene. Notes should also be made of the camera's position, characteristics, and the weather conditions that affect the camera's settings.

The next step in the process is the search of the crime scene area which presents various problems, especially when the area is extensive. It is essential that proper consideration be given to all aspects of the search problems before proceeding, in order that the search can be made as complete and as thorough as possible. The general organization of the search party will be determined by the size and type of the area to be covered, available personnel, and the equipment with which the party must work. It is important that the search party be divided into manageable units with each unit aware of just what area it is responsible for searching.

The number of men necessary to conduct a search will largely depends on the conditions existing at the time. Search parties may consist of as many as a hundred men, but should never be less than two. Regardless of how many people conduct the search, a careful and methodical effort must be exerted, the search should proceed according to plan, and the searchers should search for one thing at a time. If the search is going to be for fingerprints then the search should be for fingerprints only until they are all found or there is good reason to believe that there are none. Then the search can be for bloodstains or hair, and so on down the line. The searchers may note the presence and location of one piece of evidence while looking for another piece, but the evidence noted should not be touched until the searchers are specifically looking for it. It is also a good practice to have each man responsible for a particular duty during the search. He can be a note taker, sketcher, evidence collector, or whatever else is necessary. Then when the search starts again he should be switched to another duty. This helps keep the persons alert, and insure adequate coverage of the scene. Never search a crime scene just once; always go over and over the scene until everyone is satisfied that all the evidence has been found. However, do not handle evidence more than is necessary.

The Identification of Evidence

To insure the proper chain of custody of any evidence found during the search it is necessary that every piece of evidence be marked for identification by the person who found it. Others who witness its finding should also mark the evidence of witness. If the evidence does not provide sufficient suitable area for more than a single mark it should be marked by the finding officer and witnessed by other persons. The characteristics of the mark should be recorded in the notes of the officer as well as the witnesses.

The following steps should be followed in the marking of any evidence:

1. Each bit of evidence should be appropriately marked at the time it is removed from its original position. No piece of evidence should be removed from the position in which it was found until after it has been photographed, sketched, processed for latent fingerprints, and listed in the investigator's notebook.

2. The mark "X" should never be used to identify evidence. The identifying mark should be one that is characteristic and easily identifiable. Using the written initials of the finder is considered best. The mark used and its position as well as any serial numbers or distinctive marks present on the object should be recorded in the officer's notebook for further reference.

3. Whenever possible mark the object itself, taking extreme care to prevent any destruction of the value of the evidence. Unless evidence or the article itself prohibits it, the marks made on all articles of a similar nature should be in the same direction.

4. Always mark the container in which the object is being placed as well as the object. If the object cannot be marked then seal the container and mark the seal as well as the container.

Proper marking and the keeping of notes on the evidence found during the course of an investigation will make it possible for the officer to positively identify each piece of evidence at the time it is presented in court. Using a mark which is characteristic and one that will not have been accidentally placed on the evidence, as well as knowing just where to locate the mark on the evidence is of great value to the officer witness. He will be poised and confident in his manner of handling the evidence and the judge and jury will be more impressed as to the value of the evidence presented.

Preservation and transportation of Evidence Preservation

Each article of evidence should be placed in an appropriate container depending on the nature and size of the evidence. It is recommended that the container used should be larger than necessary to normally accommodate the evidence article, so as to prevent it from being crushed or squeezed by other articles. However, the container should not be so large as to cause damage to the evidence from excessive movement. The containers should be new and clean and each article of evidence should be packed in a separate container. This is especially necessary where evidence might have foreign matter adhering to it. Should any matter adhering to the evidence fall or become separated from the article during or after packing, it will be found in the container in which the article was packed.

Transporting the Article

The transportation of the sealed evidence to the laboratory should be accompanied by the officer who collected the evidence. It has to be shipped to a laboratory, the safest and most practical method of delivery should be used and in the case of perishables, the speediest method possible should be employed.

The contents of any container should be clearly listed on the package or label. If several individual packages are packed into a single large container, the larger container should be labeled to show the content of the individual containers. This would be in addition to the labels on the individual containers. The information contained on the package should include: (1) contents of the package, (2) name of the person from whom the property was taken or where it was found, (3) the number of the case on which the evidence has a bearing, (4) the date and time it was found, (5) the name of the officer who found or received it and (6) the article to be subjected to laboratory examination, and (7) the type of examination suggested.

Storage of Evidence

One of the most important phases of maintaining the value of the evidence is its storage. The evidence must be stored in such a manner that there is no question as to actual possession.

In some departments the officer has to store the evidence in his personal locker, in others, special wall lockers are set aside for the storage of evidence with keys only available to the officer in charge of each watch and the officer who has evidence to store.

Probably the best arrangement would be for the department to have a property room with an officer from each watch in charge. After obtaining evidence the officer could then place it in the property room and receive a receipt for it. This room should have the proper facilities for storing evidence along with a strict security apparatus to keep all people except the officer of each watch in charge of it from entering.

This way the evidence could be properly stored according to its needs and the officer can be assured that the evidence has been under strict control and carefully guarded until it is needed in the laboratory or in the courtroom. He can then maintain the chain of evidence and assure the court and jury the evidence was given the best of care and handled by responsible personnel.

Conclusion

The identification, collection, and preservation of evidence are of crucial importance to the execution of police responsibilities. The auxiliary policeman will be expected to take part in these duties when the occasion arises. His specific duties will naturally depend upon the department with which he is allied. However, in most departments because of the presence of specialists in the area of criminal investigation his main duties will be the protection of the scene and assisting the specialists where necessary. Regardless of what his duties are, the auxiliary policeman should constantly strive to gain further knowledge about this field for his own benefit. In a natural or manmade disaster he may be the only representative of the law left within an entire area and, at that time, his knowledge of proper investigative techniques will help continue law and order in society.

The auxiliary officer should remember that there are always clues at a crime scene and that everything within a crime scene is significant. Only knowledge, experience, and patience will bring these clues into the open and these take time to develop. He should never forget the importance of maintaining the chain of custody by issuing and receiving receipts. Above all, he should be constantly aware of the importance of evidence and should constantly try to improve his own skills in its identification, collection, and preservation.

www.ingramcontent.com/pod-product-compliance
Lightning Source LLC
Chambersburg PA
CBHW082206300426
44117CB00016B/2691